Better Homes and Gardens.

HEARTS
to Stitch & Craft

© 1984 by Meredith Corporation, Des Moines, Iowa.
All Rights Reserved. Printed in the United States of America.
First Edition. Second Printing, 1984.
Library of Congress Catalog Card Number: 83-61322
ISBN: 0-696-01085-2 (hard cover)
ISBN: 0-696-01087-9 (trade paperback)

BETTER HOMES AND GARDENS® BOOKS

Editor: Gerald M. Knox
Art Director: Ernest Shelton
Managing Editor: David A. Kirchner

Crafts Editor: Nancy Lindemeyer
Senior Crafts Books Editor: Joan Cravens
Associate Crafts Books Editors: Debra Felton,
    Laura Holtorf, Rebecca Jerdee, Sara Jane Treinen

Associate Art Directors: Linda Ford Vermie,
    Neoma Alt West, Randall Yontz
Copy and Production Editors: Marsha Jahns,
    Mary Helen Schiltz, Carl Voss, David A. Walsh
Assistant Art Directors: Harijs Priekulis,
    Tom Wegner
Senior Graphic Designers: Alisann Dixon,
    Lynda Haupert, Lyne Neymeyer
Graphic Designers: Mike Burns, Mike Eagleton,
    Deb Miner, Stan Sams, D. Greg Thompson,
    Darla Whipple

Vice President, Editorial Director: Doris Eby
Group Editorial Services Director: Duane Gregg

General Manager: Fred Stines
Director of Publishing: Robert B. Nelson
Vice President, Retail Marketing: Jamie Martin
Vice President, Direct Marketing: Arthur Heydendael

Hearts to Stitch and Craft
Crafts Editors: Debra Felton, James A. Williams
Copy and Production Editors: Nancy Nowiszewski,
    Carl Voss
Graphic Designer: Mike Burns
Electronic Text Processor: Cynthia Kalwishky
    McClanahan

TABLE OF CONTENTS

HEARTS
for Someone Special

Who can resist the appeal of hearts? This beloved motif has long been a symbol of romance and hospitality among friends and loved ones. With that in mind, we've assembled a book full of heart projects to stitch and craft for your home, family, and friends using your favorite techniques and materials.

The collection begins with valentines to craft for someone you love. The four cut-paper cards shown here are made from old-fashioned postcards, doilies, and trims. For stitchers, there is a delicate needlepoint pansy gift tag, below; a cross-stitched design, below right, on perforated paper; and a tatted heart, above right. For other romantic treasures, please turn the page. Instructions for the cards begin on page 10.

♥ *Designed as a bridal arrangement, the delicate dried flower bouquet, opposite, makes a glorious surprise for anyone on your gift list. Rows of dried statice, rosebuds, and bachelor's buttons are glued to a heart-shape plastic foam base, then accented with ribbons and lace.*

Best friends, little sisters, and sweethearts alike will treasure the elegant keepsake box, right. Begin with a plain candy box, then add satin, a heart-shape paper doily, and pretty floral appliqués. Personalize the gift with a gold-letter message.

The two handsome woodburned boxes, below, make a sentimental yet practical gift. Even if you never have tried woodburning, you'll find it simple to decorate purchased craft boxes with the folk art design or overall heart pattern shown here.

♥Romantic enough for sweethearts, and lovely enough for the most special of family and friends, these keepsakes are as fun to make as they are to give.

The heart sachets, above and left, are stitched from snippets of subtly patterned fabrics and trimmed with lace ruffles and cutouts, floral appliqués, seed pearls, and bits of embroidery.

To individualize each sachet, start with a basic heart shape, then widen, lengthen, or even double it, as shown at left. After stitching, fill the hearts with a fragrant mixture of dried flowers and herbs that you make yourself (see instructions on page 25).

If you're experienced at working with wood, you can craft the graceful heart frame, opposite, from a piece of mahogany or other fine wood. To complete the frame, add a slightly padded, fabric-covered, heart-shape mat. You'll find no nicer way to display a treasured photograph of your loved ones.

Needlepoint
♥ PANSY

shown on page 4

MATERIALS
5-inch square of petit-point canvas
Marlitt floss in the colors listed
   in the color key, *below*
Stiff cardboard
Beige and purple papers
12 inches of ¼-inch-wide ecru lace

INSTRUCTIONS
The petit-point design is worked
in about the same way as a design
using a larger canvas. However,
to work with the petit point canvas, make a frame by cutting a 4-
inch square from the center of a
piece of cardboard. Tape the edges
of the canvas to the frame.

Following the chart and color
key, *below*, work the design, centering it on the canvas. Use two
strands of floss and basket-weave
stitches throughout.

To assemble the card, cut a 4x8-
inch rectangle from beige paper
and a 3½-inch square from purple. Fold the beige paper in half
crosswise to form the card.

From the card front, cut out a
heart shape that is slightly larger
than the needlepoint design. Lay
the pansy behind the opening and
the purple square over the back.
Glue the edges to the card front.

Glue lace along the opening on
the card front; punch a hole in the
card to make a gift tag, if desired.

Tatted
♥ VALENTINE

shown on page 5

MATERIALS
For tatted heart, see ornament
   materials, page 52
Burgundy, pink, blue paper
Gold braid
White lace trim

INSTRUCTIONS
To make the tatted heart, follow
the instructions on page 52. From
burgundy paper, cut a heart
shape that extends ¼ inch beyond
the tatted heart. From a piece of
pink paper folded in half, cut a
heart that is ½ inch larger on all
sides than the burgundy one.
Place the top curves of the heart
along the fold in the pink paper to
form a hinge for opening the card.

Glue the burgundy heart to the
front of the pink card. Add gold
braid, lace, and paper trim. With
dabs of glue, secure the tatted
heart to the front of the card. Add
an easel stand to the back.

Cut-Paper
♥ GREETINGS

shown on pages 4-5

MATERIALS (for all four cards)
Poster board; construction paper
   in a variety of colors
Assorted gift wraps
Paper lace doilies
Antique-looking stickers
Motifs from greeting cards,
   catalogs, and magazines
Old photographs
Gold or silver stick-on letters
Scraps of satin, laces, and ribbons
Small sprays of artificial flowers
Gold paint; fine paintbrush
Watercolor paper, paints, brushes
Spray adhesive; white glue
Bits of ½-inch-thick plastic foam

INSTRUCTIONS
"On the Wings of Love" card
At right back in photograph.

Cut the center from a heart-
shape paper doily; glue the remaining lace frame to gold paper.
Back the paper with cardboard.
Decorate the frame with flower
motifs. Cut out the entire frame,
leaving a ⅛-inch border of gold.

Cover a square of poster board
with floral paper. Frame it with
edging cut from a square doily.

Frame a small photograph with
paper mats. Glue a block of plastic
foam to the back of the photograph, then glue the block to the
center of the square card. Mount

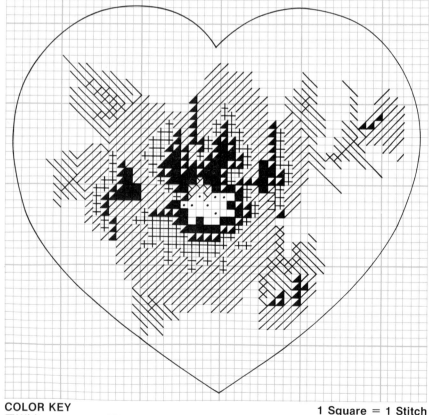

COLOR KEY

☐ White	■ Black	⊞ Lavender
⊡ Light Gray	◢ Dark Blue	⊠ Green
⊠ Yellow Orange	◿ Turquoise	◹ Light Green

1 Square = 1 Stitch

the heart-shape frame on three small blocks of foam and center it over the photograph. Glue the frame in place.

Complete the card by backing cutouts of butterflies, cherubs, birds, and other motifs with cardboard, foil, and blocks of foam; glue in place around the heart. Add an easel stand to the back.

Heart-in-hand card
At left front in photograph.

On watercolor paper, trace around your hand; cut out the shape. Cut out the outlines of a heart from the palm of the hand, but leave the heart connected to the palm.

Paint the hand beige and the heart pink. Decorate the hand and heart with seals; pen a message around the heart.

Cut the center from a square paper doily and edge the remaining frame with gold paint. Glue the frame to a folded square of construction paper.

Center the hand on the card; glue it in place. Add decorative seals, photographs, or scraps of lace. Trim the hand with a cuff of paper lace, bits of foil, and a bow.

"True Love" card
At right front in photograph.

Clip out the center of a square paper doily and glue the lacy edging to a gold foil backing. Cut out the frame, leaving a narrow border of gold. Center the frame on folded construction paper and glue it in place.

Decorate the card with flower seals, a cutout of hearts and arrows, and bows. Use a gold pen to write a message around the heart, if desired.

"My Heart is Thine" card
At left back in photograph.

Cut away the center from a large heart-shape doily. Mount the remaining lace frame on gold paper and cut it out, leaving a narrow rim of gold around the inner and outer edges.

Glue the frame to construction paper. Cut the paper into a heart shape and glue it to cardboard. Edge the card with gold paint.

Add a cherub cutout, foil letters, and flowers to the card, as desired. Glue an easel stand to the back.

Cross-Stitched
"BE MINE"
shown on page 5

MATERIALS
6-inch square of perforated paper
Embroidery floss in the colors listed in color key, *below*
Maroon, purple, gold paper
Tapestry needle

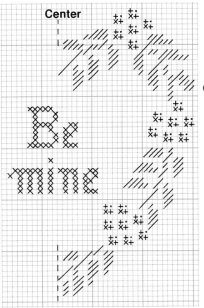

1 Square = 1 Stitch

COLOR KEY
☑ Green   ⊞ Violet
☒ Red   ⊡ Red-Violet

INSTRUCTIONS
To work with perforated paper, hold it in your hands, or tape it between stretcher strips. Use a blunt tapestry needle, two strands of floss, and light stitch tension. If you rip the paper, use clear fingernail polish to repair it.

Starting 3 inches from one side of the paper and 1 inch from the bottom, begin stitching the bottom point of the heart, following the chart and color key, *above.*

The chart shows half of the heart design and all of the lettering. Flop the heart motif along the center line to complete the left half of the design.

To assemble the card, fold in half a 7x13-inch piece of maroon construction paper. On the front, draw a heart shape that is ¼ inch

bigger all around than the cross-stitched heart design. Cut out the heart from the paper.

Cut a 6⅛x6½-inch piece of gold paper and a 6x6⅜-inch piece of purple. Center the purple paper on the gold; glue them together.

From the middle of the paper, cut a heart that is ¼ inch bigger all around than the maroon cutout. Center the purple-gold sheets on the card front; glue in place.

Trim the stitchery to fit inside the card so that the design shows through the front. Tape the perforated paper in place.

Satin-Covered
CANDY BOX
shown on page 6

MATERIALS
Heart-shape candy box
Heart-shape paper doily
½ yard of pink satin
Scrap of quilt batting
Floral print wrapping paper
Gold braid or other trim
Gold paper letters
Small floral appliqués
White glue; spray glue
Gold paint; fine brush

INSTRUCTIONS
Glue a layer of quilt batting to the top of the box lid. Cut a piece of satin 1 inch larger all around than the box top. Glue the margin of the fabric to the sides of the box top, smoothing the fabric in place. Clip and overlap the excess fabric where necessary.

Cut a strip of fabric 1 inch wider than the height of the box lid and long enough to go all the way around, plus ½ inch for overlap.

Turn under ¼ inch on the top edge of the fabric strip and glue the fabric around the sides of the box top, positioning the folded edge to hide the raw edges of the top piece of fabric.

Turn the lower edge of the side strip to the inside of the lid; glue in place. Conceal the seam along the top rim of the box lid with a row of gold braid.

continued on page 12

From the heart-shape doily, clip away the center portion and excess edging to make a piece that will fit on the box top, as shown in the photograph on page 6. Outline the inside and outside edges of the paper heart with gold paint.

Lightly coat the back of the doily with spray glue, then put small dots of white glue along the edges to make sure the paper will lie flat against the fabric. Let the glue dry until tacky, then position the paper on the fabric box top and smooth it into place.

Glue floral appliqués around the paper heart. Use paper letters to spell out a message or initials inside the doily; secure the letters with dabs of white glue.

To line the inside of the box, cut a piece of floral gift wrap to lie flat in the bottom of the box. Secure it in place with spray glue.

Cut a strip of paper to fit around the inside edge of the box and glue it in place with spray adhesive. Finish the top and bottom inside edges with rims of gold paint.

Woodburned
♥ **TRINKET BOXES**
shown on page 6

MATERIALS (for both boxes)
Unfinished wooden craft boxes
Woodburning tool
Sandpaper
Graphite paper
Graph paper
Acrylic paint or fabric dye
Paintbrush
Clear acrylic spray

INSTRUCTIONS
General woodburning directions: Woodburning tools come with different types of tips. The designs shown can be made with a basic tip, but experiment on a scrap of wood until you achieve a consistent pressure and the desired line thickness.

Before you begin woodburning, sand the wood surface smooth and remove any dust. Lightly pencil a freehand design on the box or use graphite paper to transfer the pattern, *below,* to the wood.

When the woodburning is completed, sand the box lightly. Referring to the photograph for ideas, add splashes of color by diluting acrylic paints or mixing a weak solution of fabric dye and applying it to the box with a brush.

If desired, spray the finished box with clear acrylic.

Folk art box
Enlarge the pattern, *below,* onto graph paper. Lay graphite paper on the box top and tape the graph paper design over it so the pattern is centered. Trace over the design with a sharp pencil to transfer it to the box.

1 Square = ½ Inch

With the woodburning tool, outline the heart, then burn a solid ¼-inch border around the edges. Make the dots in the box top by pressing the tip of the tool into the wood, then turning it. Form the leaves with the side of the tool.

To decorate the sides of the box, burn dots every ½ inch along the upper and lower edges, then make a solid ¼-inch-thick border along the lower edge of the box.

Box with overall design
Draw 1-inch squares diagonally on the box top and sides, then draw a heart inside each diamond. Burn in the lines, then create the hearts by using the side of the tool to burn one side of the heart at a time.

Keepsake
♥ **FLORAL BOUQUET**
shown on page 7

MATERIALS
8-inch square of ½-inch-thick plastic foam
8-inch square of white felt
Dried statice, rosebuds, roses, and bachelor's-buttons
25-inch lengths of ⅛-inch-wide satin ribbon
1 yard of 1-inch-wide satin ribbon
7 inches of 1-inch-wide white grosgrain ribbon
2 yards of 1-inch-wide lace
¾ yard of ⅜-inch-wide braid
Fabric glue; white glue
Craft knife

INSTRUCTIONS
Enlarge a heart pattern from this book so that it measures 8 inches from top to bottom and 7½ inches across at the widest points. Pencil the pattern onto plastic foam, then cut out the foam heart with a craft knife. This will form the base of the bouquet.

Glue the ⅜-inch-wide braid to the side of the foam, overlapping the ends at the top inside point. Pin the braid in place until it is completely dry.

To the outside edge of the heart front, glue the 1-inch-wide satin ribbon, gathering it slightly as you go and positioning it so the edge of the ribbon extends out over the heart. Pin the ribbon in place until dry.

Atop the ribbon, glue ½-inch-wide lace. Trim off any excess lace and set it aside.

To fill in the heart with flowers, first refer to the photograph on page 7 to see how the rows of flowers begin at the edge of the lace and work in toward the center.

Glue statice to the foam for the first row, rosebuds for the second, and statice for the third. Add another row of lace, and fill in the center with more rows of alternating statice and rosebuds.

To add dimension to the heart, glue an arrangement of rosebuds and bachelor's-buttons atop the center of the heart so that the inner row of lace shows.

Tie the lengths of narrow ribbon into bows and tack them to the center top of the heart.

From white felt, cut a backing the same size as the foam heart. Make a handle by stitching the ends of the grosgrain ribbon to the back of the felt, leaving the ribbon loose so it can be grasped easily. Then glue the felt to the back of the heart and let dry.

If you like, lightly scent the bouquet with rose oil.

Lace-Trimmed
♥ SACHETS

shown on page 9

MATERIALS
Scraps of fabric
Assorted lace trims, braid, beads, and satin ribbons
Small artificial flowers
Potpourri

INSTRUCTIONS
Referring to heart-shape patterns in this book and the photographs on page 8, draw a heart pattern that is about 3 to 4 inches high. For variety, experiment with different shapes. For instance, double the pattern to make twin hearts, elongate the curved edges of the heart, or lengthen the straight edges to make a more vertical shape.

Adding ¼-inch seam allowances, cut a pattern from tissue paper. Then cut two pieces for each heart from fabric scraps. With right sides facing, stitch the pieces together, leaving an opening for turning. Trim the seams and clip the curves every ⅛ inch.

Turn the heart right side out and fill it with potpourri. Stitch the opening closed.

Referring to the photographs for ideas, embellish the sachet by tacking gathered laces around the edges. Glue braid or twisted pearl cotton on top of the lace. Add gathered-ribbon rosettes and artificial flowers, ribbon streamers, bows, beads, or other trims.

Sweetheart
♥ PICTURE FRAME

shown on page 8

MATERIALS
One 9x11-inch and one 4x9-inch piece of 1-inch-thick mahogany
8-inch square each of heavy cardboard and hardboard
8½-inch square each of fabric and quilt batting
Jigsaw; rabbeting bit; router
Sandpaper; ½-inch brads
Stain or varnish
Graph paper; graphite paper

INSTRUCTIONS
Enlarge the pattern, *right*, onto graph paper, flopping it along the center line. Mark the dash and dot-dash lines on the right half only. The solid lines represent the pattern for the front of the frame, and the broken lines will be used when making a back brace.

With graphite paper, transfer the pattern to mahogany. Cut out the design with a jigsaw; use the rabbeting bit and router to make a ⅜-inch groove in the back of the frame for the mat and picture. Sand the frame until smooth.

To make the pattern for the back brace, you will need to alter the full pattern. First, cut the enlarged pattern in half. Discard the left side, leaving only the portion shown in the pattern, *right*.

On your enlarged pattern, cut away the short lower right leg of the frame between the two dot-dash lines so that only the tall, question-mark-shape portion remains. Fold the pattern so the two dotted lines meet. This will shorten the piece to the proper height for the back brace.

Trace this altered pattern onto mahogany; cut out the brace with a jigsaw. Sand smooth. Stain or varnish the frame and back brace as desired.

To make a mat for your photograph, first cut a piece of heavy cardboard to fit inside the frame. Slip the board behind the frame and lightly sketch in the shape and size that the picture should be

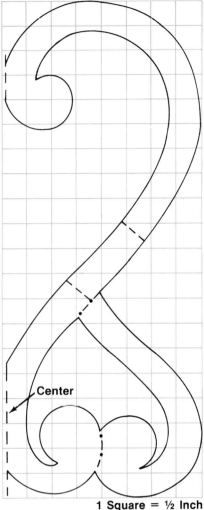

1 Square = ½ Inch

so that there is about a 1-inch margin of cardboard along the sides. Cut out this inner heart shape from the cardboard.

Cut a piece of batting and fabric the same size as the mat, adding ½-inch seam allowances to the inner and outer fabric edges. Glue the batting to the mat.

Lay the fabric over the padding, clip the seam allowance along the curves, and turn the excess fabric under the edges of the mat. Tape or glue the fabric to the back to secure it in place.

Position the photograph and mat in place. Cut hardboard to fit into the frame. Lay it atop the mat; hold it in place by driving brads into the back of the frame.

Center the brace against the back of the frame so that the wide curve is at the bottom. Glue the top of the brace in place, leaving the bottom free.

EASY HEARTS
to Make and Give

♥ *Making special heart projects for yourself or others needn't be time-consuming or difficult. Here is a selection of things to make that is simple enough for beginners (some even are tailored to children), but satisfying enough for more experienced crafters. Projects such as the woven basket or cross-stitched sewing accessories shown on the next 12 pages are ideal for bazaars. And the appliquéd crib quilt, knitted stocking cap, and woodcrafter's box are delightful gifts for babies, children, and adults.*

The cross-stitched floral motif shown here makes a pretty pocket, or can be adapted to an ornament, sachet, or pillow. Instructions for this and other crafts begin on page 16.

Flowered
♥ **POCKET EMBROIDERY**
shown on page 15

MATERIALS
10-inch square of hardanger fabric
10-inch square of cotton fabric
¾ yard each of lace, ribbon
Embroidery floss in the colors listed in the color key, *below*
Embroidery hoop; needle
Water-erasable transfer pen

INSTRUCTIONS
To work the rose motif, first find the center of the hardanger and the center of the design on the chart, *below*.

Following the chart and color key, stitch the design from the center out. Use four strands of floss and work over two threads of the fabric.

Note: See page 56 for information on perfecting your cross-stitched projects.

When the embroidery is complete, press the fabric on the wrong side.

With water-erasable pen, trace a heart shape around the stitchery, leaving at least ¾ inch of fabric beyond the outermost stitches. Cut out the heart.

To line the pocket, cut a piece of fabric the same size as the front. With right sides together, stitch the front to the lining, using a ¼-inch seam allowance and leaving an opening for turning. Clip the curves, then turn the heart right side out and press it well. Slipstitch the opening closed.

To attach the heart pocket to a skirt, pinafore, apron, or other item, baste lace and ribbon around the edge of the pocket back, if desired. Then pin the heart in place and topstitch it ¼ inch inside the heart.

The rose motif also makes an attractive heart-shape ornament or sachet when worked over one thread of hardanger. This will reduce its size by half, making it suitable for a 3½-inch-high heart.

Quick-to-Knit
♥ **CHILD'S HAT**

Keeping your child warm is easy when you knit this perky stockinette-stitch cap. Though it's made in just one size, the hat is simple to custom fit using elastic inserted in the hem. To create a delightful winter ensemble, knit this traditional folk art motif into a matching sweater, scarf, or mittens.

MATERIALS
One 50-gram skein of red Phildar Prognostic yarn and ½ skein of white, or suitable substitutes
½-inch-wide length of elastic to fit around head
Sizes 1 and 3 knitting needles, or sizes to obtain gauge, *below*

Gauge: With larger needles over st st, 13 sts = 1 inch.

Abbreviations: See below.

INSTRUCTIONS
With smaller needles and red, cast on 140 sts. Work even in st st for 1 inch.

Change to larger needles and work in st st (k one row; p one row) 1¼ inches, ending with a p row.

Join white and, referring to the chart, *below*, work the heart pattern. (*Note:* When changing colors, twist the new color around the color in use to prevent making holes in work.)

Work 21 rows of two-color pattern. Drop the white. Work even

Chart #1.

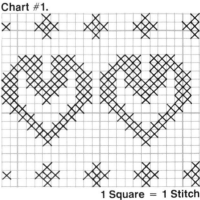

1 Square = 1 Stitch

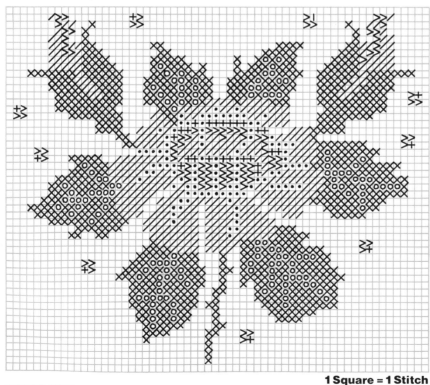

1 Square = 1 Stitch

COLOR KEY:
+ Gold	/ Light rose	✕ Dark green
> Pale pink	• Dark rose	o Light green

in st st for 3 inches past pattern, ending with a p row.

Top shaping: * K 2 tog. Rep from * across—70 sts. Break yarn and draw tail through sts. Pull tightly and fasten.

Blocking: Dampen the hat with cool water and lay it on a folded sheet. Using rustproof pins, secure the hat to the towel, keeping the tension even and smoothing any wrinkles.

Cover the hat with a damp, lint-free cloth. Set your iron at a moderate temperature and press the hat slowly and gently. Remove the cloth and let the hat dry for at least eight hours.

Finishing: Turn 1 inch at lower edge to inside and sew in place to form hem. Sew the back seam, leaving an opening at the inside of the hem.

Insert elastic in the casing formed by the hem; fit it to the proper head size. Overlap the ends of the elastic and stitch them together. Close the casing with matching yarn.

Make a white pompon by wrapping yarn about 50 times around a 2-inch-wide cardboard strip. Remove the yarn, tie it in the center, and trim the ends. Sew the pompon to the top of the cap.

KNITTING ABBREVIATIONS

beg	begin(ning)
dec	decrease
inc	increase
k	knit
MC	main color
p	purl
pat	pattern
psso	pass slip st over
rem	remaining
rep	repeat
rnd	round
sk	skip
sl st	slip stitch
sp(s)	space(s)
st(s)	stitch(es)
st st	stockinette stitch
tog	together
yo	yarn over
*	repeat from * as indicated

Ribbon-Trimmed
♥ BELT AND BAG

Smart fashion accessories such as these make any occasion a celebration. Styled from glistening moiré taffeta and crisp plaid ribbon, this elegant evening purse and belt are surprisingly simple to make.

MATERIALS (for both projects)
1 yard each of red moiré taffeta, lining fabric, lightweight fusible interfacing, and double-faced 1-inch-wide black satin ribbon
4½ yards of ⅛-inch-wide gold metallic ribbon
7 yards of 1½-inch-wide plaid taffeta ribbon
2 sets of hook and eye fasteners
Gold thread

INSTRUCTIONS
Purse
On tissue paper, draw a heart pattern that is 9 inches high and 9 inches across. Cut two hearts each from the taffeta, lining fabric, and interfacing. Cut one 2½x20-inch gusset each from taffeta, lining, and interfacing.

Fuse the interfacing to the wrong side of each taffeta heart and gusset strip. Machine-stitch gold ribbon to the right side of each taffeta heart, positioning it ½ inch from the raw edges and mitering the ribbon at the inside and outside points of the heart.

Cut two 58-inch lengths of plaid ribbon. Stitch together the ends of each strip, making two continuous loops of ribbon.

Gather each of the ribbon loops by basting as close as possible to one edge. Pull up the gathering threads, then pin each gathered loop to the right side of one taffeta heart, ¼ inch from the raw edge. Baste the ribbons in place.

Stay-stitch the gusset ⅜ inch from the long raw edges. Clip to the stay-stitching.

Fold the gusset in half crosswise and mark the center with a pin. With right sides together and matching the pin marker to the bottom point of one taffeta heart, pin the gusset to the heart.

Stitch, using ½-inch seam allowances, and starting and stopping 1 inch from the raw edges of the gusset at the top inside point of the heart.

Note: As you stitch, be careful not to sew over the gold ribbon on the right side of the heart, or to catch the gathered ribbon in the stitching.

Repeat the process, sewing the other side of the gusset to the second taffeta heart. Trim the seams, clip curves, and turn the purse right side out.

Stay-stitch the lining gusset and sew it to the lining hearts as directed for the taffeta hearts, leaving an opening along one straight side. Clip curves.

Slip the lining over the bag, right sides together, and pin it in place. Using a ½-inch seam allowance, stitch the lining to the bag around the top opening, matching the raw edges of the gussets and hearts. Trim seams; clip curves.

Pull the bag through the opening in the lining, then slip-stitch the opening closed. Press the lining to the inside of the bag through the top opening.

Stitch black ribbon handles to the bag at the top opening. Then stitch an 18-inch length of gold ribbon to each end of the gusset at the top to tie the bag closed.

Belt
Enlarge the pattern, *right*, onto brown paper, extending the ends of the belt until the pattern is 2 inches longer than your waist measurement. Cut one piece each from taffeta, lining, and interfacing. Fuse interfacing to the wrong side of the taffeta.

Stitch gold ribbon to the right side of the taffeta, positioning it ½ inch from each long raw edge. Miter the ribbon at the inside and outside points of the center front.

Cut two lengths of plaid ribbon, each twice the measurement of the belt length. Turn under ¼ inch on the raw ends and stitch.

Machine-stitch a row of gathering stitches along one long edge of each ribbon. Then fold each ribbon in half crosswise and mark

the center point with a pin. Pull up the gathering stitches.

Matching the pins to the upper and lower center front points of the belt, pin the ruffles in place, right sides together, along both long edges of the belt. The edge of each gathered ruffle should be ¼ inch from the long edges of the taffeta, and the ends of the ruffle should be ½ inch inward from the short ends of the belt. Stitch the ruffles in place.

Pin the lining to the belt, right sides together, so that the gold ribbon and ruffle are not caught in the stitching line. Stitch, using ½-inch seam allowances and leaving an opening along one short side.

Trim the seams; clip curves and clip into the inner point of center front. Turn the belt right side out and slip-stitch the opening closed. Attach hook and eye fasteners.

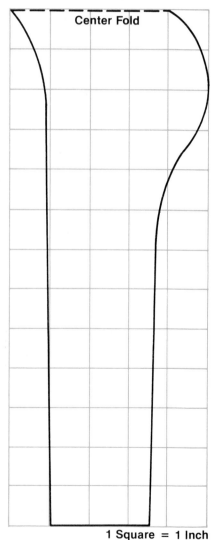

Center Fold

1 Square = 1 Inch

Beginner's
♥ CROSS-STITCH

Introduce your child to a lifetime of crafting with the cross-stitched pincushion, needle case, sewing bag, and carryall shown here. Stitched on Aida cloth with bright-colored flosses, the designs are simple, yet attractive and functional, too.

MATERIALS (for all projects)
12x18 inches of 14-count ecru Aida cloth
Embroidery floss in desired colors
2½ yards of ecru piping
1 yard of 45-inch-wide blue quilted nylon
½ yard of iron-on interfacing
½ yard of 45-inch-wide muslin
3x7 inches of gold felt
Polyester fiberfill
Two 12-inch purse handles
Embroidery hoop
Water-erasable transfer pen

INSTRUCTIONS
General directions: To fit all the projects onto the Aida cloth, use a water-erasable pen to mark off the following areas: For the pincushion, 4x4 inches; needle case, 5x9 inches; sewing bag, 4½x8 inches; tote bag, 4½x10½ inches. Complete all the cross-stitching before cutting apart the fabric.

The pattern, *right,* is one-fourth of the finished motif. To complete the design, flop the pattern three times. (*Note:* It may be helpful to chart the entire design on graph paper, using pencils in the colors of your floss.)

To begin stitching, use a waste knot to anchor the thread end in the Aida cloth. With three strands of floss, work each stitch over two threads of fabric. Work all crosses in the same direction.

After finishing with a length of floss, clip off the waste knot and weave the ends under the stitches. Then, when finished stitching, use a warm iron to press the fabric lightly on the wrong side, cushioning the embroidery on a layer of soft towels.

Pincushion
Work one motif, centering it in the 4-inch area of Aida cloth. Cut out the square and trim it to 3½ inches. Cut a 3½-inch square of muslin for the pincushion back.

With right sides facing and using a ¼-inch seam allowance, sew the front and back together, leaving an opening. Turn the pincushion, stuff it firmly with fiberfill, and blindstitch it closed.

Needle case
Embroider one motif on the right half of the 5x9-inch rectangle. Trim the rectangle to 4½x8½ inches; bond the back with fusible interfacing. On the right side, using ½-inch seam allowances, sew piping around the edges. Cut a 4½x8½-inch muslin lining.

With right sides facing and leaving an opening, sew the lining to the needle case along the piping seam line. Trim seams, clip corners, and turn. Press the needle case and sew the opening closed.

Glue gold felt inside the needle case and insert needles into the felt. Fold the case in half.

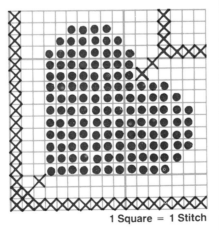

1 Square = 1 Stitch

Sewing bag
Work two adjacent patterns into the 4½x8-inch area, deleting the inside borders and leaving two squares between motifs. Cut out the rectangle; bond the back with interfacing. Sew piping to the long sides of the rectangle ½ inch from raw edges. Fold the raw edges to the back and press. Set aside.

From quilted nylon, cut one 8x20-inch rectangle for the bag and one 4x5½-inch piece for a hanging loop. Cut a 4x5½-inch muslin loop lining.

At one end of the 8x20-inch rectangle, center and cut away a 3¾x5-inch opening. Trim the raw edges of the opening with piping, then fold the edges back and topstitch. Pin the cross-stitched band 1 inch below the opening, matching the side raw edges. Topstitch the band ¼ inch from all edges.

With right sides facing, fold the nylon pocket in half crosswise and sew the sides together ½ inch from the raw edges; turn.

Trim the long sides of the hanging loop with piping. With right sides together, sew the loop to the lining; turn right side out and press. Make several tucks in the top of the bag to fit the hanging loop. Sew the loop to the bag.

Carryall
Work three adjacent motifs in the 4½x10½-inch area, deleting borders and leaving spaces between the motifs as for the bag. Stitch piping to the long edges.

From quilted nylon, cut a 10½-inch square for a pocket and an 11x34-inch piece for the tote. Cut an 11x34-inch muslin lining.

With right sides facing, pin the embroidered band to one edge of the pocket; stitch together along the piping stitching line. Press the seam toward the band, then topstitch the band above the piping.

Fold the 11x34-inch carryall piece in half crosswise with wrong sides facing. Turn under ½ inch along the bottom of the pocket, then position the pocket on the carryall front 1½ inches above the fold and topstitch it in place.

Fold the carryall in half crosswise, right sides facing. Using ½-inch seam margins, stitch the sides together, beginning at the fold and stitching 9 inches on each side. Repeat for the lining.

Turn the carryall right side out; leave lining unturned. Slip the lining inside, matching raw edges. Fold the raw edges inside and slipstitch the lining to the carryall front and back.

Fold over 1½ inches along the tops of the carryall; sew the edges to the inside to form casings for the handles. Insert the handles, gathering the carryall slightly, and glue on the handle ends.

Embroidered
♥ **FOLK-ART PILLOW**

Not all hearts are sweet and frilly valentines. This vibrant pillow, for example, was inspired by the simple lines, strong colors, and rich textures of traditional European peasant embroideries. You can craft this hearty Old World accent for your own home with simple appliqués and couching stitches worked on brilliant red wool.

The height of the finished pillow is 14 inches.

MATERIALS
½ yard of red wool
Ecru 3-ply Persian wool
Scraps of blue and ecru felt
One package of ecru piping
Tapestry needle
Polyester fiberfill
Fabric glue
Dressmaker's carbon paper
Graph paper
Tracing paper

INSTRUCTIONS
Enlarge the pattern, *below*, onto graph paper. (*Note:* The pattern does not include seam margins.)

On the right side of the wool, position the pattern so that there is at least ½ inch of fabric around the edge of the heart and so an equal amount of fabric remains for the back of the pillow.

With dressmaker's carbon paper, transfer the pattern to the fabric, including all design lines.

The shaded portions of the pattern indicate placement of the felt appliqués. Using your enlarged pattern as a guide, cut out four blue leaves, six blue dots, and four ecru hearts from felt. Do not add seam allowances to these pieces.

Position the appliqués on the pillow front and use small dabs of fabric glue to secure them in place.

To embroider, or "couch," the yarn design on the pillow front, first pull one ply from a length of three-ply yarn.

Knot the end of the single ply and thread it through a tapestry needle. Draw the needle from the back of the fabric to the right side along the design at the center top of the heart.

To couch, lay the remaining 2-ply yarn along the design lines marked on the pillow front and, at ¼-inch intervals, stitch over it with the one-ply yarn to hold it in place. (See the diagram, *below*.)

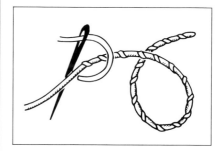

When you reach the end of a length of yarn or it is no longer needed, draw it to the underside of the pillow front and knot it close to the fabric to hold it in place. Continue with another length, beginning by bringing the yarn up from the back.

When you have finished stitching the design, cut out the heart from the fabric, adding ½-inch seam allowances all around. From the remaining wool, cut another piece the same size for the back of the pillow.

On the right side of the pillow front, pin the piping so that it lies

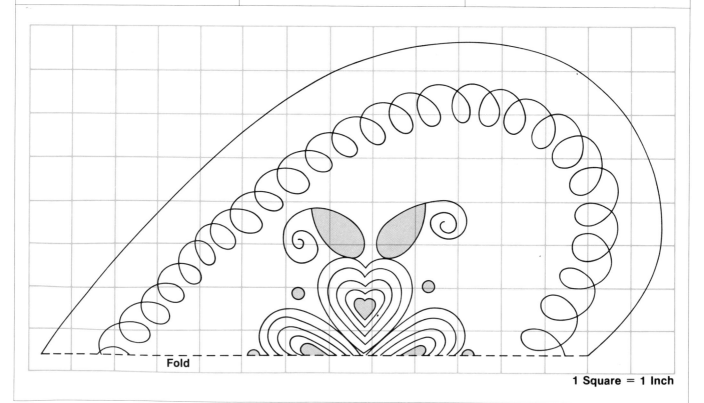

Fold

1 Square = 1 Inch

just inside the stitching line and so the raw edges are toward the outside. Overlap the ends of the piping along one straight edge. Then baste the piping in place.

With right sides together, pin the pillow front to the back. Using a zipper foot, stitch the two pieces together, sewing as close as possible to the piping and leaving an opening for turning.

Turn the pillow right side out and stuff it lightly. Slip-stitch the opening closed.

You can adapt this pattern to pockets, ornaments, sachets, or other projects by varying the size. To reduce the finished pattern, make the grid squares smaller than 1 inch. Or trace the pattern in its existing size.

Woven
♥ **RUSH BASKET**

From a teenager's art equipment to an executive's office supplies, there's no limit to the uses for this handy woven catchall. The basket is so easy to make, you'll want to weave several to use as gifts for all ages.

MATERIALS

Approximately 120 yards of 3/16-inch-wide sisal, or other supple fiber
Length of coat hanger wire

INSTRUCTIONS

The basket is 4½ inches high.

Cut sisal into twenty 10-inch lengths; these will be the warp cords. Cut the remainder into 4-foot lengths for weaving.

Divide the shorter lengths into two bundles of 10 cords each. Lay one bundle perpendicularly atop the other. Hold one end of a weaver cord on the center top of the top bundle as shown, *below.*

Working over and under, wrap the weaver cord around the center cross three times. (See drawing, *below.*) Then spread out the cords so they lie side by side like spokes in a wheel.

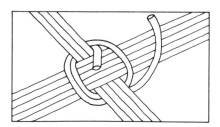

With the weaver cords, weave over and under the spokes, separating them in pairs and spacing them evenly. (See the drawing, *above right.*) You will have 10 pairs of spokes emanating from the center.

Continue weaving until the work measures 2 inches from the center. To end the weaving, separate the last pair of spokes and work the weaver over one, then under one to prevent overlapping. The bottom now is completed.

To weave the sides of the basket, invert the bottom of the basket so that the spokes hang down. Rejoin the two spokes you separated as you completed the bottom. Then, working with two weavers at the same time, place one weaver over and one weaver under the same pair of spokes. (See the drawing, *below.*)

Twist each weaver once between each pair of spokes. Then place the weaver from beneath the previous spoke over the next

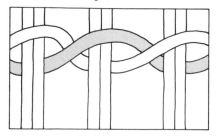

one and the weaver from above the previous spoke underneath the next one.

To begin a new weaver, place one end under the pair of spokes the previous weaver went under and leave the tail on the inside.

Keep the weavers and spokes woven tightly together, forcing the spokes into a heart shape as you go. Keep weaving the sides until they are 4½ inches high.

To finish the top edge of the basket, bend the end of a length of coat hanger wire into a hook. Hide the ends of the last weavers by using the hook to pull the ends over and under the spokes on the inside of the basket. Cut the ends short.

To finish the ends of the spokes, first force the hook up through the top two weavers on the outside of the basket.

Hook the spokes to the left and pull them down through the weavers, leaving the tails on the outside.

Move the hook to the next spoke and do the same, repeating the process until all the spokes are pulled through. Trim the ends of the spokes.

Woodcrafter's
♥ TRINKET BOX

A few tools, a beautiful piece of soft wood, and some simple woodworking skills are all you need to make this graceful treasure box. Standing 4½ inches high, the box has a swivel lid that swings back to reveal your favorite trinkets.

For a special friend, make the box an extra-thoughtful gift by filling it with a fragrant herbal potpourri. You'll find a recipe for a favorite scent below.

MATERIALS

Six ¾ x5x5-inch pieces of soft wood (such as pine, basswood, or yellow poplar)
Wood glue
Jigsaw; band saw
Drill with ⅜-inch-diameter bit
Drum sander
3-inch length of ⅜-inch-diameter doweling
Sandpaper; triangular file
Compass; graph paper
Paint or stain

INSTRUCTIONS

The box is made by cutting out the interior from four of the wood pieces, then stacking and gluing them together. Finish by adding the bottom of the box and the lid and cutting out the heart shape.

Enlarge the pattern, *below*. On each of the wood pieces, draw the heart shape, positioning it in the same place on each piece.

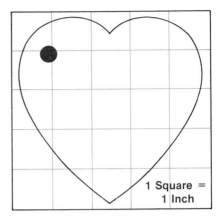

1 Square = 1 Inch

With a compass, draw a 2¾-inch-diameter circle in the exact center of four of the hearts. Drill a hole inside each circle; slip the jigsaw blade inside this hole. Cut out the circles with a jigsaw. Glue together the four pieces; let dry thoroughly. Sand the hole with a drum sander.

Glue on a fifth piece of wood for the bottom of the box. Let dry. Then lay the sixth piece (lid) on top and drill a ⅜-inch-diameter dowel-hinge hole (indicated on the pattern) through the lid and into the box to a depth of 3 inches.

Place a few drops of glue in the bottom of the dowel hole; drive in the 3-inch dowel. Sand the dowel flush with the top of the lid.

With the band saw, cut out the box along the heart outline, holding the two pieces together firmly. Sand the box, using a triangular file on the point of the heart. Paint or stain the box as desired.

To make a Garden Herb potpourri, combine ⅛ cup each of sweet marjoram and dried mint leaves with 1 tablespoon each of thyme, rosemary, whole cloves, and cinnamon. Add 1 teaspoon each of caraway seed, allspice, cardamom, and dried orange rind.

Place 1 tablespoon of orrisroot atop the herbs; add two drops of bergamot oil to the orrisroot. Let the mixture stand for two minutes; gently blend the ingredients.

To cure the potpourri, pour it into a lidded jar and let it stand for six weeks in a dark closet.

Appliquéd
♥ CHILD'S COMFORTER

Soft, colorful, and washable, too, this bright velour quilt is ideal for babies and toddlers. And at 35x42½ inches, it's just the right size for a tiny tot.
Appliqué hearts to the background blocks by hand or machine—whichever suits you best. Then trim some of the hearts with lace (as shown) or braid, and finish with colorful ribbon bows.

MATERIALS
2⅔ yards of 44-inch-wide white velour
¼ yard each of assorted colors of velour
Quilt batting
4 yards of grosgrain ribbon
10-inch lengths of ribbon in assorted colors
7½ yards of ¾-inch-wide ecru lace or narrow braid
Cardboard or coffee can lids
Water-erasable pen

INSTRUCTIONS
To begin, preshrink all fabrics. From cardboard, cut a precise 7½-inch square to serve as a template for cutting the blocks.

From paper, cut a heart shape that will fit comfortably in a 7-inch square, then cut the shape for a template from cardboard or a coffee can lid.

Note: If hearts are to be machine-appliquéd, do not add seam allowances. For appliquéing by hand, add a ¼-inch seam margin around the edge of the template.

Using the square template, cut 18 squares from the white fabric. Also from white fabric, cut ten 8¼x8¼x11¾-inch side triangles and four 6¼x6¼x9-inch corner triangles. Trace and cut 18 hearts from assorted colors.

Pin and baste each heart to a square so that the bottom of each heart points toward one corner of the square.

To machine-appliqué, set the machine on a close zigzag stitch and sew along the edges of the heart with thread that matches the heart fabric. For hand-appliqué, turn under ¼ inch around the edge of each heart and press, clipping the seam allowance to lie flat. Pin the hearts to the squares and blindstitch in place.

Referring to the photograph for the arrangement of colors and using ½-inch seam allowances throughout, assemble the quilt top in six rows, as follows:

Row 1: Lay out one square, right side up, so the point of the heart points down. Stitch a corner triangle to the upper left side of the square. Join a side triangle to the lower left side and upper right side of the block.

Row 2: Join three heart blocks in a diagonal row by sewing upper right and lower left sides together. Finish the row by joining side triangles to the lower left side of the lower heart block and to the upper right side of the upper heart block. Join the upper left edge of Row 2 to Row 1.

Row 3: Repeat Row 2, *except* join five heart blocks together instead of three; add a corner block to the upper right side of the upper heart block instead of joining a side triangle. Join to Row 2.

Row 4: Join five heart blocks as for Row 3; sew a corner triangle to the lower left of the lower heart block and a side triangle to the upper right of upper heart block.

Row 5: Same as Row 2.

Row 6: Same as Row 1, *except* sew a corner triangle to the lower right side instead of upper left.

Press the seams open. Cut two 2¾-inch-wide border strips long enough for the top and bottom of the quilt. With right sides together, sew them to the edges of the quilt top. Then cut two 2¾-inch-wide borders for the sides and stitch them to the quilt.

From white velour, cut a backing the same size as the quilt top. Lay the quilt top against the backing, right sides together, and place the batting, cut to fit, on top.

Pin the layers together and sew around all sides, leaving a 12-inch

opening for turning. Turn the quilt right side out and slip-stitch the opening closed.

At 4-inch intervals, baste or pin through the quilt. Then, using white thread, hand- or machine-quilt along the seam lines of the squares and border.

Tack lace and ribbon or braid along the seam lines of the border. Sew lace or braid around some of the hearts, then stitch ribbon to each heart and tie it into a bow.

APPLIQUÉ TECHNIQUES
Whether you appliqué by hand or machine, you can produce expert results by following these tips.

To keep appliqués from stretching, back them with a scrap of fusible interfacing. If you're stitching by hand and will be turning under the edges, cut the interfacing without seam allowances. For machine appliqué, cut the backing the same size as the pattern piece.

If you're working with appliqués that are too small to pin or baste in place, use a scrap of fusible webbing to hold them to the background fabric while you sew. Iron the webbing into place, using a press cloth.

When appliquéing by machine, you can make sharp corners by first zigzag-stitching to the corner. Leave the needle in the fabric at the outside of the line of stitches, then lift the presser foot and pivot the fabric. Lower the presser foot and begin sewing so the first stitch goes toward the inside of the design, overlapping the stitch just made. Continue, working slowly and smoothly.

To make a rounded edge on a hand-stitched appliqué, cut the shape in its *finished* size from a piece of paper. Lay the paper on the wrong side of the fabric appliqué, leaving an even seam allowance on all sides.

Press the edge of the fabric over the paper, then baste through all thicknesses and press firmly with an iron. To sew the appliqué in place, remove the basting stitches and paper pattern, and stitch along the creased edge.

HEARTS
for the Home and Hearth

♥ Crafters have long known that hearts add a feeling of warmth and hospitality to a home. As the projects in this chapter illustrate, the simple heart shape can turn a functional item into something special. Following the instructions on the next few pages, you can stitch a quilt and embellish it with painted or appliquéd hearts, crochet subtle heart motifs into elegant edgings, or build an heirloom cradle and paint it with a heart-shape wreath of flowers. Whichever project you choose, the results will make your home more inviting.

To begin, try your hand at one of the projects, opposite. The patchwork afghan is knitted in stockinette stitch and edged with a crocheted border. The place mats are painted and varnished like the floorcloths of colonial times. And the child-size "courting" chair is painted with a portion of the motif used on the place mats. For instructions, please turn the page.

Knitted
♥ **PATCHWORK AFGHAN**

shown on page 29

MATERIALS

Unger Roly Poly yarn (or suitable substitute): 5 balls aqua, 3 balls purple, 2 balls each of pink, gray-green, lavender, and kelly green
Size 11 knitting needles, or size to obtain gauge given below
Size I aluminum crochet hook

Gauge: With 2 strands held tog over st st, 3 st = 1 inch; 4½ rows = 1 inch.

Abbreviations: See page 17.

INSTRUCTIONS

The afghan is worked with two strands of same-color yarn held tog except when indicated otherwise. It has 20 blocks worked in four strips of five blocks each.

Refer to the charts, *right,* for the block with three hearts, eight hearts, a single heart, and diagonal stripes.

Each block is 31 sts across and 39 rows from top to bottom, plus two extra rows of garter sts on the top and bottom of each strip.

Edge the afghan with crochet.

First Strip: Keep 1 st at right-hand edge and 2 sts at left-hand edge in garter st throughout.

First Block: With lavender, cast on 31 sts. Work in garter st for 4 rows. Work 6 rows in st st, keeping right-hand st and left-hand 2 sts in garter st (see chart for indicated garter sts).

Refer to single-heart chart, *right,* and beg with Row 9 on chart, work heart motif with 1 strand of pink and 1 strand of aqua held tog; use lavender for background color. Complete all 23 rows of heart motif; drop pink and aqua. With lavender, complete 6 rows more st st, then work 2 rows more in garter st.

Second Block (checkerboard pat): *Row 1:* With 2 strands aqua k 10, with 2 strands kelly green k 11, with 2 strands aqua k 10.

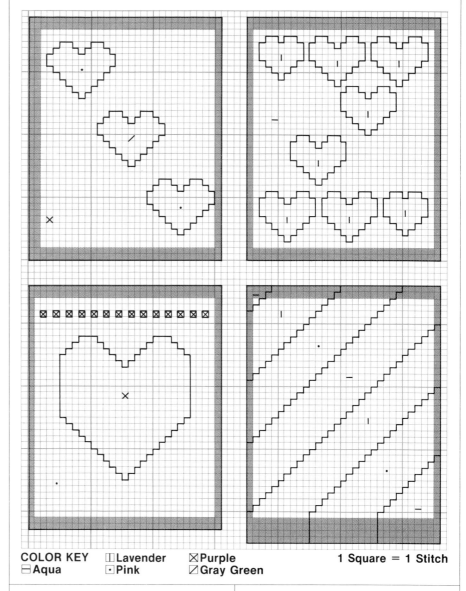

COLOR KEY
⊟ Aqua ⊞ Lavender · Pink ⊠ Purple ⊘ Gray Green
1 Square = 1 Stitch

Row 2: Rep Row 1. *Row 3:* K 10 aqua, k 11 kelly green, k 10 aqua.

Row 4: K 2 aqua, p 8 aqua, p 11 kelly green, p 9 aqua, k 1 aqua. Rep Rows 3-4 four times more; rep Row 3 once.

Next row: K 2 kelly green, p 8 kelly green, p 11 aqua, p 9 kelly green, k 1 kelly green. Keeping in alternating color sequence established, work 12 rows more in st st, keeping garter sts as established.

Following row: Rep Row 3.

Next row: Rep Row 4. Rep Rows 3-4 four times more; rep Row 3. In alternating color sequence, work 2 rows more garter st.

Third Block (3-heart block): With purple, follow chart for 3-heart block, *above,* keeping garter sts at each edge as established.

Work hearts in pink and green as indicated. Complete Third Block with 2 rows garter st.

Fourth Block: With 2 strands lavender, work 2 rows garter st. Keeping garter sts at each edge as established, work st st for 35 rows. Work 2 rows garter st.

Fifth Block: Work as for First Block. Use gray-green for background, work heart in aqua. End with 4 rows garter st. Cast off.

Second Strip: *First Block:* With 1 strand purple and 1 strand gray-green held tog, cast on 31 sts. Work in garter st for 4 rows. Keeping 1 st at each edge in garter st, work in st st for 35 rows. Work 2 rows garter st.

Second Block: Work as for First Strip, First Block, using pink for background, and working heart in purple. End with 2 rows garter st.

Third Block: With 2 strands kelly green, work as for First Strip, Fourth Block, except beg st st panel with a p row for reverse st st. End with 2 rows garter st.

Fourth Block: With 1 strand aqua and 1 strand pink held tog, work 2 rows garter st. Keeping 1 st at each edge in garter st, work 11 rows st st. Continue with 2 strands lavender held tog for 13 rows. Finish block with 1 strand aqua and 1 strand pink held tog, ending with 2 rows garter st.

Fifth Block: With 2 strands pink, work 2 rows garter st, 35 rows st st, 4 rows garter. Cast off.

Third Strip: *First Block:* With 2 strands of each held tog, cast on 10 sts aqua, 11 sts pink, and 10 sts lavender. Work in garter st in colors established for 4 rows. Referring to chart, *opposite,* work in diagonal stripe pat, keeping 1 st at each edge in garter st.

Second Block: With purple, work 2 rows garter st, 35 rows st st, 2 rows garter st.

Third Block: With aqua, work 2 rows garter st. Referring to 8-heart block chart, *opposite,* work heart motifs over next 35 rows. Work 2 rows garter st in aqua.

Fourth Block: Work as for First Strip, First Block. Use pink for background, work heart in kelly green. End with 2 rows garter st.

Fifth Block: With 1 strand purple and 1 strand gray-green, work 2 rows garter st, 35 rows st st keeping 1 st at each edge in garter st, and 4 rows garter st. Cast off.

Fourth Strip: *First Block:* Work as for First Strip, First Block, using purple for background, working heart in pink, and keeping 2 right-hand-edge sts and 1 left-hand-edge st in garter st. End with 2 rows garter st.

Second Block: With 1 strand aqua and 1 strand gray-green held tog, work 2 rows garter st, 35 rows keeping edge sts in garter st as established, 2 rows garter st.

Third Block: Work across in garter st for 2 rows in following order: 1 strand pink and 1 strand gray-green over first 10 sts, 1 strand lavender and 1 strand pur-

ple over next 11 sts, 1 strand pink and 1 strand green over rem 10 sts. Keeping edge sts in garter st and all sts in stripe as established, work 35 rows st st. Work 2 rows garter st in stripes as established.

Fourth Block: With purple, work 2 rows garter st, 35 rows st st, 2 rows garter st, keeping edge sts in garter st as established.

Fifth Block: Work as for Fourth Strip, First Block, using aqua for background, and working heart in lavender, and keeping edge sts as established. End with 4 rows garter st. Cast off. Sew strips tog.

Edging: *Rnd 1:* Join 2 strands aqua in any corner, ch 2, 2 sc in same sp; sc around, making 3 sc in each corner; join, ch 2. *Rnd 2:* Sc in each sc around, making 3 sc in each corner.

Rnd 3: Ch 3, in same sp work (dc, ch 1, 2 dc), * sk 3 sc, (2 dc, ch 1, 2 dc for shell) in next sc. Rep from * around, taking care to have a shell in each corner.

Rnd 4: Rep Rnd 3. *Rnd 5:* Rep Rnd 3, making (2 dc, ch 1, 2 dc, ch 1, 2 dc) in each corner. Fasten off.

Hearts-and-Flowers
♥ **STENCILED PLACE MATS**

MATERIALS
13x19-inch piece of canvas
Beige latex paint
Acrylic paint in dark green, light green, turquoise, pink, lavender, and purple
Tracing paper
Graph paper
Fine-tip paintbrush

INSTRUCTIONS
The place mats, shown in the photograph, *below left,* are made by coating canvas with latex paint, then painting the hearts-and-flowers design.

Enlarge the pattern, *below,* onto graph paper, flopping it along the center line. Trace the pattern onto tracing paper.

Center

1 Square = 1 Inch

Cover the canvas with two coats of latex paint. Let it dry thoroughly. Line up the straight edges of the hearts-and-flowers pattern with the edges of the canvas and transfer the design lines to the place mat.

Note: Instead of transferring the design to the place mat, you can cut a stencil for the design from paper or plastic, then tape the stencil to the canvas. Refer to stenciling information on page 35.

To paint the design, use the photograph, *left,* as a color key. Dampen the brush, then dip it lightly in paint. Wipe the excess paint on a paper towel, working the paint up into the bristles. Apply the paint sparingly, outlining each design element, then filling it in. Let the paint dry thoroughly.

Coat the painted place mat with a layer of clear acrylic, if desired.

The hearts-and-flowers motif, or portions of it, adapts well to other types of craft projects. The design can be appliquéd, quilted, embroidered, or treated with other colors and techniques.

continued on page 32

Built-for-Two
♥ **CHILD-SIZE CHAIR**

shown on page 29

MATERIALS

4x8 feet of ½-inch-thick particleboard
2 feet of 2x2-inch pine
2 feet of 1x1-inch pine
3 feet of ¾x1-inch pine
1- and 1½-inch-long finishing nails
Sandpaper
Wood putty
Wood glue
Primer paint
Pale green semigloss latex enamel paint
Acrylic paints for design
Graphite paper

INSTRUCTIONS

Referring to the diagrams, *below and right*, lay out the pieces on the particleboard. Because there is no grain direction to the board, you may lay out the pieces in any direction to conserve space.

Begin assembling the chair by nailing and gluing the ends to the front and back pieces. Rip the pine 2x2 diagonally to make a brace for each corner of the chair. Nail and glue the braces in place so they are flush with the top and bottom edges of the legs.

Next, insert the center leg unit (see diagram, *right*), and glue and nail it in place. Rip the 1x1 pine diagonally, as you did with the 2x2, to make four corner braces. Nail and glue these to the center leg unit and the front and back.

Cut three 1x¾-inch arm caps with a ½-inch radius on the front ends. Nail and glue them to the tops of the ends and the center leg unit. The center cap should be flush with the front and back edges, which makes it 11½ inches long. The end caps overhang ½ inch on opposite edges, making them each 12 inches long.

Position the seats in place and glue to secure. Nail down through the seats and through the ends into the seat edge.

Attach the hearts, centering them on the back of each seat. Countersink all visible nail heads and fill them with wood putty. Sand all surfaces and round edges.

Prime the chair and, when dry, finish with two coats of semigloss latex enamel, sanding lightly between the coats.

To paint the motifs onto the seat: On graph paper, enlarge the heart motif from the place mat pattern, *page 31,* using a scale of 1 square = 1¾ inches. Enlarge the center top tulip motif using a scale of 1 square = 2 inches.

Referring to the photograph on page 29 for placement, transfer the designs to both sides of the heart-shape chair backs, using graphite paper. Paint with acrylics, following the photograph for a color key.

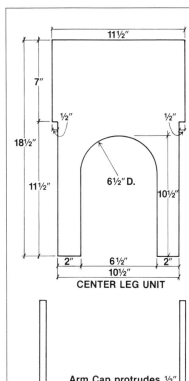

CENTER LEG UNIT

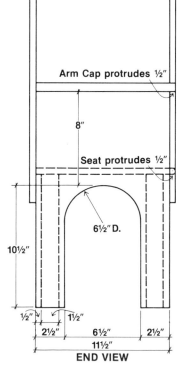

END VIEW

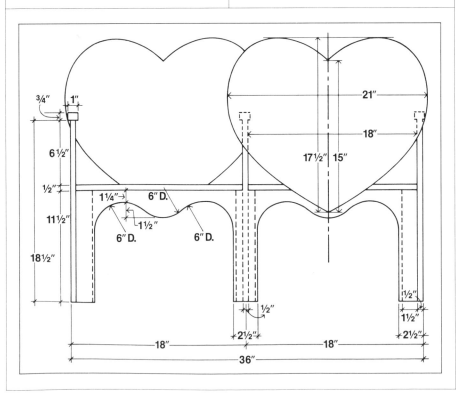

Heart-Trimmed
♥ GRAPEVINE WREATH

When you think of grapevines, chances are you envision rustic country charm. But this wreath, painted pristine white and accented with flowers and pastel hearts, is enchantingly elegant in any setting. Its simplicity makes it exceptionally versatile—change the color or leave it natural, if you like, or create your own arrangement of flowers, ribbons, and trims.

MATERIALS

Several 12- to 20-foot lengths of mature grapevine no more than ½ inch in diameter
Garden clippers
Light-gauge wire
Scraps of ½-inch-thick pine
Jigsaw or coping saw
Drill with ¼-inch bit
White acrylic paint
Acrylic paints or fabric dyes in assorted colors
⅛-inch-wide satin ribbon
Dried or silk flowers

INSTRUCTIONS

To find wild grapevines, look along fencerows and around the outskirts of hardwood forests. The vines should be brown, not green. They are most easily pulled from late summer through fall.

With clippers, trim the grapevines, leaving intact as many small tendrils as possible. Remove any loose bark.

Working with one vine at a time, bend each length into a wreath shape. Entwine the vines, one atop another, until the wreath is 3 to 4 inches thick.

Weaving the vines together will usually hold them in place. But to make them more secure, wrap them with thin light-gauge wire or monofilament.

Paint the wreath with white acrylic or another color, as desired. Let dry completely.

To make the wooden hearts that hang from the wreath, cut a paper pattern of a heart that will fit onto your pine scraps. Trace around the pattern onto the pine. Using a ¼-inch bit, drill a hole through the top of each heart. Use a jigsaw or coping saw to cut out the heart shapes.

Paint the hearts with acrylics or immerse them in fabric dyes; let them dry completely. Pull a length of ribbon through the hole in each heart and tie the ribbon to the wreath. If you wish, decorate the wreath with ribbon streamers and bows, dried or silk flowers, or other trims.

Painted
♥ **HEART QUILT**

Using heart motifs and fabric painting techniques, you can brighten your bedroom with this colorful quilt. Design your own blocks by arranging different-size hearts in a pleasing combination. Then choose one of several methods of painting on fabric to complete the 42x57-inch coverlet and an array of matching pillows.

MATERIALS
Quilt
4½ yards of pink fabric
1½ yards of white fabric
Pillow
1 yard of pink fabric
½ yard of white fabric
Pillow form
For both projects
Fabric paints; brushes
Stencil paper and brushes or
   block-printing equipment
Polyester quilt batting
Craft knife

INSTRUCTIONS
Quilt
Cut seventeen white and eighteen pink 8½-inch-square blocks. On paper, design a motif for the white blocks, using hearts in several sizes.

The easiest way to paint the white fabric squares is to draw heart shapes onto the right side of the fabric and fill in the outlines with acrylic or fabric paints. But for a more uniform look, stencil or block-print the design.

Stenciling: Using a craft knife, cut heart shapes from stencil paper or plastic. Spread the white fabric squares over a pad of newsprint to absorb excess paint, then secure the stencils to the fabric with masking tape.

To paint, dip the stencil brush in a small amount of paint and blot it on a paper towel. Holding the brush vertically, apply the paint in a circular motion, rubbing until the stencil area is covered with a light coat of color.

When the paint is dry, heat-set it by pressing the fabric lightly on the wrong side, using a medium-hot iron.

Block printing: You'll need small linoleum blocks, an assortment of carving tools, and a printer's brayer; all are available from an art supply store.

To carve the design, use carbon paper to trace the heart shape onto the linoleum surface. Gouge out all the material around the heart design. When printed, the heart will appear as a solid image.

Lay out the fabric squares on newsprint. With the printer's brayer, apply a thin, even coat of paint to the surface of the block. Press the block on the fabric using a smooth, even pressure. Lift the block straight up to remove.

Reink the block for each print; wipe the block clean when the linoleum becomes caked or tacky.

Heat-set the paint when dry.

Assembling the quilt: Alternate the white and pink squares in seven vertical rows of five blocks each. Stitch the blocks together using ¼-inch seam allowances.

To make the border, cut eighty 4x4-inch pink squares. With wrong sides facing, fold each square in half once to form a rectangle; press. Fold the top corners down and to the center so the raw edges meet, creating a triangle.

With right sides facing, pin the triangles to the edges of the quilt top, overlapping them slightly to fit. Machine-stitch them in place.

Cut the quilt batting and a pink backing the same size as the quilt top (minus the border triangles). Place the right sides of the fabric together; pin the batting to the top. Machine-stitch around three sides. Turn, keeping the batting flat. Slip-stitch the opening closed.

With white thread, hand- or machine-quilt around each painted heart. In each pink block, quilt an outline of a large heart.

Pillow
Use a 14-inch white square for the top and a pink square for the back. Cut a piece of batting and backing for each. Paint the pillow as you did the quilt. Quilt the front and back.

With right sides facing, stitch the front to the back along three sides. Turn; insert the pillow form, and slip-stitch closed.

Homespun
♥ CROCHETED EDGING

This filet-crocheted edging of hearts and fans turns a plain napkin into an attractive homespun accessory. Work the subtle design in ecru thread, as shown, or use a crisp, bright white cotton.

MATERIALS
One 350-yard ball of ecru Knit Cro-Sheen or suitable substitute
Size 5 steel crochet hook
13-inch square of linen fabric

Gauge: 8 hdc = 1 inch.

INSTRUCTIONS
Make four strips as follows: Ch 99.
Row 1: Sc in 2nd ch from hook and in each ch across. Ch 4, turn.

Row 2: Sk 1st 2 sc, hdc in each of next 2 sc, * ch 2, sk 2 sc, 1 hdc in each of next 2 sc, rep from * to end with sk 2 sc, hdc in turning ch, ch 2, turn.

Row 3: 2 hdc in 1st sp, ch 2, 2 hdc next sp, hdc next hdc, * ch 1, sk next hdc, 2 hdc next sp, (ch 2, sk next 2 hdc, 2 hdc next sp) 2 times, ch 1, sk next hdc, hdc next hdc, 2 hdc next sp, (ch 2, sk 2 hdc, 2 hdc next sp) 2 times, hdc next hdc, rep from * to end with 2 hdc in last sp, ch 4, turn.

Row 4: 2 hdc in 1st sp, * hdc in each of next 3 hdc, hdc next sp, (ch

2, sk next 2 hdc, 2 hdc next sp) 2 times, ch 2, sk 2 hdc, hdc next sp, hdc in each of next 3 hdc, 2 hdc next sp, ch 2, sk next 2 hdc, 2 hdc next sp, rep from *, end with 2 hdc in last sp, ch 2, sk last 2 hdc, hdc in turning ch, ch 2, turn.

Row 5: 2 hdc in 1st sp, * hdc in each of next 6 hdc, 2 hdc next sp, (ch 2, sk 2 sc, 2 hdc next sp) twice, hdc in each of next 6 hdc, 2 hdc next sp, rep from * across row, end with 2 hdc in last sp, ch 2, turn.

Row 6: Dc in 1st 10 hdc, * 2 dc in next sp, ch 2, sk 2 hdc, 2 dc next sp, dc in 18 hdc, rep from *, ending with dc next 10 hdc, ch 2, turn.

Row 7: Hdc in 1st 10 dc, * ch 2, sk 2 dc, 2 hdc in next sp, ch 2, sk 2 dc, hdc next 18 dc, rep from *, end with 10 dc, ch 2, turn.

Row 8: Hdc in 1st 8 hdc, * ch 2, sk 2 hdc, hdc next sp, ch 1, hdc same sp, ch 2, dc in next hdc, ch 1, dc next hdc, ch 2, in next sp work, (hdc, ch 1, hdc, ch 2). Sk next 2 hdc, hdc next 14 hdc, rep from * ending with 8 hdc, ch 2, turn.

Row 9: Hdc in 1st 6 hdc, * ch 2, sk 2 hdc, sk ch-2 of previous row, (hdc next hdc, ch 1) 2 times, in next sp work hdc, ch 1, hdc; ch 1, (dc next dc, ch 1) 2 times, in next

CROCHET ABBREVIATIONS

beg	begin(ning)
bet	between
ch	chain
cont	continue
dc	double crochet
dec	decrease
dtr	double treble
hdc	half double crochet
inc	increase
lp(s)	loop(s)
pat	pattern
rep	repeat
rnd	round
sc	single crochet
sk	skip
sl st	slip stitch
sp	space
st(s)	stitch(es)
tog	together
yo	yarn over
*	repeat from * as indicated

sp work, hdc, ch 1, hdc; (ch 1, hdc next hdc) 2 times; ch 2, sk next 2 hdc, hdc next 10 hdc, rep from * ending with 6 hdc, ch 2, turn.

Row 10: Hdc in 1st 4 hdc, * ch 2, sk 2 hdc, sk ch-2 of previous row, (hdc in next hdc, ch 1) 4 times, in next ch-1 sp work, (hdc, ch 1) twice, (dc in next dc, ch 1) twice, in next ch-1 sp work, (hdc, ch 1) twice, (hdc in next hdc, ch 1) 4 times, ch 1, sk ch-2 and next 2 hdc, hdc in next 6 hdc, rep from *, ending with hdc in next 4 hdc, ch 2, turn.

Row 11: Hdc in 1st 2 hdc, * ch 2, sk 2 hdc, sk ch-2 of previous row, (hdc in next hdc, *ch 3, sl st in 3rd ch from hook—picot made*, hdc next hdc, ch 1) 3 times, dc next dc, make picot, dc next dc, ch 1, (hdc next hdc, make picot, hdc next hdc, ch 1) 3 times, ch 2, sk ch-2 of previous row and next 2 hdc, hdc in each of next 2 hdc, rep from * ending with 2 hdc. Fasten off.

Corners (to be worked after all 4 strips have been completed): Lay 2 strips to be joined at right angles (right side facing up), matching rows of sc (Row 1). Attach thread to corner sc in right-hand strip, join with sl st to corresponding sc on left-hand strips. Sl st up side of left-hand strip to top of Row 2, ch 2, turn. Sl st in corresponding st of other strip.

Row 1: Sl st up one row, ch 2, turn, in ch-2 sp of previous row, work (dc, ch 1) 2 times, ch 1, join with sl st to next row on side of strip, sl st up to position for next row, ch 2, turn.

Row 2: In ch-2 sp of previous row, work hdc, ch 1, hdc; ch 2, dc next dc, ch 1, dc next dc, ch 2, in next sp work hdc, ch 1, hdc; ch 1, join to next row of strip.

Row 3: Cont in pattern established in fan pattern used between hearts on main strips. End each row of fan pattern with ch 2, sl st in end st of corresponding row on one side of strip, sl st up one row and ch 2, turn. Cont with next row of fan pattern. (*Note:* Work an additional even row before last picot row.) Fasten off.

Weave in all loose ends, then wash and block the lace according to the care instructions, *right.*

To attach the lace to the fabric square, first lay the lace over the linen and mark the inside edges of the lace on the fabric. Using these marks as a guide, finish the edges of the fabric by machine-zigzag-stitching just *outside* the marks on the fabric.

Trim the fabric close to the stitching. Then lay the lace atop the linen; the edges should overlap slightly. With narrow stitches and matching thread, hand-sew the lace to the fabric.

CARING FOR HANDMADE LACE

When you've completed your lace, give it an expert finish by gently washing and blocking it. To wash, use a mild detergent and warm, sudsy water. Rinse the lace well, but don't rub or squeeze it. Then wrap it in a towel to absorb excess moisture.

Starch the lace if you like, using a gentle solution or spray starch. Then cover it with a damp, lint-free cloth, set your iron at a moderate temperature, and press the lace lightly, using even pressure. Let the lace dry completely.

You can also block the lace, using rustproof pins to secure it to a piece of hardboard padded with blotting paper or fabric. Let the lace air-dry overnight.

If your lace becomes stained, it can be bleached by rinsing it in a solution of lemon juice and water. Hydrogen peroxide, diluted according to directions on the container, also is a mild bleach.

To store lace for a long period of time, the most important considerations are to keep it from dampness and to pack it carefully. It should be packed loosely and kept in a cool, dry, dark place.

To pack small pieces, lay them flat and unfolded with acid-free tissue paper above and below each piece. For larger pieces, wrap a cardboard or wooden cylinder in tissue paper and loosely roll the lace around it. Wrap another layer of tissue paper around the outside of the lace and store it in a dark area.

Delicate
♥ **FILET-CROCHETED TRIM**

With all the grace of Victorian times, this handmade trim turns ordinary curtains or tablecloths into elegant decorating accessories.
To beautify your bedroom with the same look of antique lace, add these crocheted hearts to a dust ruffle or pretty pillowcase (see page 65).

MATERIALS

Coats and Clark's Big Ball
mercerized white crochet
thread, Size 30, or a suitable
substitute (a 216-yard ball
makes about 1½ feet of lace)
Size 12 steel crochet hook, or size
required to match gauge, below

Gauge: 15 dc = 1 inch; one heart
motif repeat = 3¼ inches.

Abbreviations: See page 37.

INSTRUCTIONS

To add the lace edging to curtains,
first measure the sides of the curtain panel and plan the heart repeat motif in multiples of 3¼
inches. If you wish, you also may
add lace edging to the bottom of
the curtain panel by making a
corner mesh according to the instructions below.

After you have planned the
lace, begin the heart motif at the
top of the panel and work toward
the hem. If necessary, work a par-
tial motif at the top of the panel.
Either fasten off the lace, ending
with Row 16, or work a corner
mesh block and continue across
the hem of the curtain.

If you plan to add the lace to a
tablecloth, follow the same proce-
dure to measure the length of lace
and number of repeats needed.
Then work the lace in one piece
according to the instructions below. Work one side at a time, adding corner motifs as you go. When
the lace is completed, stitch the
tablecloth fabric to the lace along
the straight side of the lace strip.

To work the lace for pillowcases, make a straight strip to fit
around the edge of each case.

For heart edging, begin with 1
strand of thread and a steel hook;
ch 54.

Row 1: Dc in 4th ch from hook
and in each of the next 2 ch—1
starting bl made; (ch 2, sk 2 ch, dc
in next ch) 5 times—5 sp made; dc
in next 3 ch, (ch 2, sk 2 ch, dc in
next ch) 10 times—10 sp made; [ch
8, turn; dc in 6th, 7th, and 8th ch
from hook, dc in last dc of previous row].

Row 2: (Ch 2, dc in next dc) 3
times; (2 dc in next sp, dc in next
dc) 3 times; (ch 2, dc in next dc) 4
times; dc in next 3 dc, ch 2, dc next
dc, (2 dc in next sp, dc in next dc) 4
times; dc in next 2 dc and in top of
ch-3, ch 3, turn.

Row 3: Sk first dc, dc in each of
next 3 dc, (ch 2, sk 2 dc, dc in next
dc) 3 times; dc in each of next 3 dc,
ch 2, dc in each of next 4 dc (ch 2,
dc in next dc) 3 times; 2 dc in next
sp, dc in each of next 10 dc, 2 dc in
next sp, dc in next dc, (ch 2, dc in
next dc) 2 times; ch 2, sk 2 dc, dc in
next dc, 3 dc in ch-8 loop; rep pat
between [ ]s of Row 1.

Refer to the chart, *below,* for
working Rows 4 through 8, making a 3-dc block for every shaded
square on the chart and making a
ch-2 space for every unshaded
square on the chart. Work the pat
that appears in [ ]s at the end of
Row 1 at the ends of Rows 5 and 7.

Row 9: Sk first dc, dc in each of
next 3 dc, ch 2 dc in next dc, (ch 2,
sk 2 dc, dc in next dc) 4 times; dc in
each of next 3 dc, (ch 2, dc in next
dc) 4 times; ch 2, sk 2 dc, dc in next
7 dc, 2 dc in next sp, dc in next dc,
(ch 2, dc in next dc) 2 times; ch 2,
sk 2 dc, dc in each of next 7 dc, 2 dc
in next sp, dc in next dc, (ch 2, dc
in next dc) 2 times; ch 2, sk 2 dc, dc
in next dc, 3 dc in ch-8 lp; [ch 4,
turn, dc in 4th dc, 2 dc in next sp,
dc in next dc].

Refer to the chart for the remainder of the pat, working the
pat bet [ ] that appears at end of
Row 9 at the ends of Rows 11, 13,
and 15. Rep Rows 1 through 16 for
pat. Determine the finished
length of lace and how many 3¼-
inch-wide repeats you'll need to
work to align with the fabric in-
sertion. Work the necessary repeats. End with Row 16.

To make a mesh corner—Row 1:
Ch 5, sk first 3 dc, dc in next dc;
(ch 2, sk next 2 dc *or* ch-2, dc in
next 2 dc) 15 times; 2 dc in last ch-
2 sp, dc in last dc, ch 3, turn.

Row 2: Sk first dc, dc in each of
next 2 dc, (ch 2, sk next ch-2, dc in
next dc) 15 times; ch 2, dc in 3rd ch
of ch-5 at beg of previous row, ch 5,
turn.

Row 3: Dc in next dc (ch 2, dc in
next dc) 15 times; dc in each of
next 3 dc, ch 3, turn. Rep Rows 2
and 3 alternately 7 times more.

Next row: Sk first dc, dc in each
dc, *and* 2 dc in every ch-2 sp all
across. Fasten off.

To begin the next side, attach
thread at the end of Row 16. Work
Row 1 of pat, making each dc at
right angles to the dc of the mesh
corner, working any clusters of dc
around the posts of the dc of the
corner mesh block.

Rep until all four sides of the
lace edging are completed. Slip-
stitch the end of the fourth side to
the end of the first side.

When the lace is completed,
wash and block it according to the
instructions on page 37 on caring
for handmade lace.

Hem or zigzag-finish the edge of
the curtain panel, pillowcases, or
tablecloth, then hand- or machine-stitch the completed lace
along the edge.

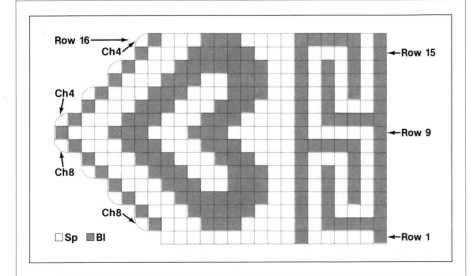

Row 16 → Ch4 → ← Row 15

Ch4 ↓

Ch8 ↑

Ch8 ↓

← Row 9

← Row 1

□ Sp ■ Bl

Pierced-Paper
♥LAMPSHADES

Made of watercolor paper painted in soft pastels, these delicately stenciled lampshades create a romantic glow.

MATERIALS
Watercolor paper
Heavy tracing paper
Brown paper; graphite paper
Lampshade rings (available at
   craft stores)
Watercolors
Craft knife; compass; glue
Spring-clip clothespins
Ribbon, braid, or velvet trim

INSTRUCTIONS
These lampshades are made from watercolor and tracing papers cut to size and then painted and pierced to create stenciled designs. Before buying the paper, make a pattern to determine the size of your lampshade and the amount of materials you'll need.

To make the pattern: The size of lampshade shapes, known as arcs, is determined by the diameter of the top of the lampshade, the diameter of the bottom, and the height.

You can make your own arc pattern by taking apart an old lampshade and tracing the shape onto watercolor paper.

Or, make a pattern for any size shade by deciding the height and diameter you want, buying the top and bottom rings, and then following these directions:

Lay out a sheet of brown paper that is at least 1 yard wide and 2 yards long (piece, if necessary). Using the diagram, *above right*, as a guide, draw a straight line 6 inches from one long edge of the paper (Line A).

Draw Line B parallel to the first line so the distance between the lines equals the desired height of the shade.

Fold the brown paper pattern in half widthwise. Open the paper and draw a line along the fold. This is Line C. Extend Line C so it is at least 3 feet long. Measure the

diameter of the top lampshade ring. Make two dots on Line B equal to the diameter, with Line C centered between the two dots. Label these dots D and E.

Measure the diameter of the bottom ring and center two dots on Line A as for Line B. Label these dots F and G. Draw a line through F and D until the line crosses C. Repeat for dots G and E. *The lines should meet on Line C.* Mark this point H.

Place a compass point on H and its pencil point on D. Draw a curved line through dots D and E. With the compass point still on H, repeat the process for F and G.

Using string, measure the circumference of the bottom lampshade ring. Lay the string on the bottom curved line of the pattern, centering it on Line C.

Mark dots at the ends of the string and draw a line from these dots to H. At one end, add ½ inch for overlap.

This is your completed pattern. Cut it out along the curved lines, disregarding lines A, B, and C.

To check the fit, clip the pattern to the rings using clothespins. Adjust the pattern if necessary.

To paint and pierce lampshade: Trace the completed arc pattern onto watercolor paper; cut out. To transfer the heart patterns, *below and above right,* to the watercolor

1 Square = 1 Inch

arc, first enlarge the two patterns. Then lay graphite paper on the arc and position the stencil pattern on top.

The pattern, *below left*, is a continuous pattern. Trace the pattern, then reposition it so that the vines are continuous. The pattern, *below,* is an individual motif

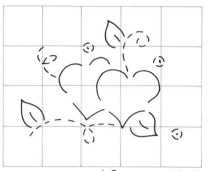

1 Square = 1 Inch

that can be repeated around the bottom of the lampshade, as shown in the photograph.

The side of the arc on which the pattern is traced will be the inside of the lampshade. On this side, paint the designs with watercolors, referring to the photograph for color ideas. Let the paint dry thoroughly.

Lay the watercolor paper over a folded towel and, using the point of a compass, pierce all the vines indicated by dashed lines in the patterns. The pierced dots should be small and evenly spaced.

To stencil-cut the hearts and leaves, lay the shade on a heavy cardboard surface. With a craft knife, cut around the shapes, leaving at least ⅛ inch of paper uncut so the designs remain attached to the shade.

On the painted side, sculpture the hearts and leaves by rolling the cut edges around a pencil. This will allow extra light to filter through the edges of the shapes.

To line the shade, trace the lampshade pattern onto heavy tracing paper. Run a thin line of glue around the outside edges on the painted side of the watercolor paper. Place the liner over the painted surfaces and let the glue dry thoroughly.

To assemble the lampshade: With the painted side of the shade toward the inside, mount the arc on the rings, using clothespins. The rings should be inside and even with the top and bottom edges of the shade.

Remove the clothespins along the area where the ends of the shade overlap. Run a thin line of glue along the overlapped edge and press the seam together. Replace the clothespins. Let the glue dry thoroughly, then remove all the clothespins.

To glue the shade to the rings, first glue the bottom inside edge of the shade to the ring and reclip with clothespins, then repeat for the top. Let dry. To finish, glue decorative trim along edges.

Appliquéd
♥ CALICO QUILT

Simple enough for beginning quilters, yet satisfying enough for experienced ones, this antique quilt is entirely appliquéd. You can stitch a replica of this charming coverlet either by hand or machine, then quilt it with outline stitches and decorative heart motifs. The finished size of the quilt shown is 65x81 inches, but you can custom-fit it by following the instructions below.

MATERIALS
2 yards of 44-inch-wide red cotton fabric
1½ yards of 44-inch-wide red cotton print
9 yards of 60-inch-wide muslin
65x81-inch batting
8 yards of white bias seam binding
Red thread; white quilting thread
Graph paper; tracing paper
Water-erasable transfer pen
Coffee can lids

INSTRUCTIONS
The quilt top is made by appliquéing 20 muslin blocks with heart motifs, setting them together on the diagonal with 12 plain muslin squares, and adding a border.

To begin, preshrink all fabrics and enlarge the pattern, *below,* onto graph paper. This will be your master pattern for cutting and positioning the appliqués.

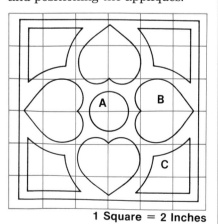

1 Square = 2 Inches

Make a template of pieces A, B, and C by tracing their outlines from the master pattern. Add ¼-inch seam allowances all around each piece and transfer these larger outlines to coffee can lids. Cut out the templates.

From cardboard, cut an 11½-inch square. This will be your template for the muslin block; it includes a ¼-inch seam margin. Also cut one triangular template that measures 11¾x11¾x16⅝ inches and one that measures 8¼x8¼x12¼ inches. These will be the half squares and quarter squares for the sides and corners.

Lay the templates on the wrong side of the fabric and trace around them with a pencil. Cut the pieces as follows:

From muslin, cut four quarter squares, 14 half squares, and thirty-two 11½-inch squares.

From solid red cotton, cut two 3x69½-inch and two 3x86-inch border strips. Cut 80 B pieces.

From red cotton print, cut 80 C pieces and 20 A pieces.

To appliqué, first trace over the outlines on the master pattern with a black pen. Then lay each of the 20 muslin squares to be appliquéd over the pattern. Using a water-erasable pen, trace the outlines on the muslin blocks.

On each A, B, and C piece, staystitch ¼ inch from the edges. Clip the curves to the stay-stitching and turn under the seam allowance; press.

Position the appliqués on the muslin squares and whip- or blindstitch them in place using thread that matches the appliqués. Stitch the appliqués to 20 muslin blocks. (*Note:* For more information on appliqué techniques, see the tip box on page 27.)

To assemble the quilt top, first lay out all the blocks and triangles on the floor and refer to the photograph to see how the squares are positioned.

Beginning in one corner, stitch a corner triangle and two side triangles to the adjacent corner square to complete Row 1. Stitch three blocks together and add a side triangle to each end to complete Row 2.

Stitch Row 1 to Row 2. Continue in this manner until all blocks and triangles are joined. Press seams to one side.

Sew the two short border strips to the short sides of the quilt top. Then stitch the long ones to the long sides.

Cut and piece backing fabric to the same size as the quilt top. Layer the backing, batting, and quilt top together and baste. Outline-quilt close to the edges of the appliqués; quilt decorative motifs in the plain blocks.

Finish the edges by sewing bias seam binding to the top of the quilt, turning it under, and blindstitching it to the back of the quilt so the binding is invisible on the quilt top.

ALTERING THE SIZE OF A QUILT
By adjusting the number and size of blocks or borders, you can easily alter the size of a quilt.

First, measure the length and width of your mattress. Then, decide if you want the quilt to reach the floor, to clear the top of a dust ruffle, or just to cover the top of the mattress. If you want a 10-inch drop, for example, add 10 inches to the foot and each side of your quilt.

To allow for enough quilt at the headboard to tuck under and go over the pillows, add 12 inches to the other end. This is a standard measurement you can use for all quilts. To allow for shrinkage caused by quilting, add 4 inches to the length and width of your quilt.

To adapt a pattern to the size you want, divide the desired width by the size of the blocks to determine how many blocks to make for each row; divide the length by the block size to determine the number of rows. Narrow or widen border strips as necessary.

You also can change the size of the quilt proportionately. For instance, if you want the quilt to be half the size of the original pattern, and the original blocks are 12 inches square, make the blocks 6 inches square instead.

Painted
♥ HEIRLOOM CRADLE

Graced with the classic styling and artistry of a treasured antique, this cradle is destined to become a family heirloom. Tole-painted garlands of flowers and ribbons frame the heart cutouts, adding an Old World touch. But besides being a beautiful first bed for baby, the cradle is convenient as well—the bars at the sides allow you to keep the cradle rocking with just a light touch of your hand.

MATERIALS
½-inch Baltic birch A-A hardwood plywood in the following dimensions: one piece 26x36 inches (headboard), one piece 22x36 inches (footboard), three pieces each 9¼x26 inches (sides and bottom)
Two 27-inch-long, 1-inch-diameter wooden dowels
Drill with 1-inch bit
Jigsaw; band saw
Rose-color latex paint
Acrylic paints in light and dark blue, light and dark green, white, pink, red, and yellow
Fine-tip paintbrush
Polyurethane
1-inch-long (2d) finishing nails
Wood glue
Wood putty
Sandpaper
Graph paper; graphite paper

INSTRUCTIONS
The pattern, *above right*, shows the outlines of the cradle's 25-inch-high headboard and 20½-inch-high footboard. Enlarge the patterns onto graph paper, flopping them along the center line and marking the shaded portions on your enlargements.

The straight shaded areas indicate where the sides and bottom are attached to the ends, the circle indicates the hole for the dowel, and the shaded heart represents

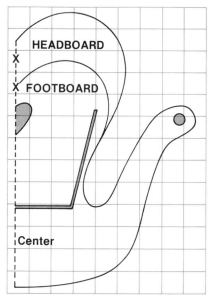

1 Square = 2 Inches

the area to be cut out of the end of the cradle. Draw the same heart on the headboard pattern between the two Xs.

Cut the enlarged patterns from the graph paper and trace them onto the appropriate pieces of birch plywood, transferring the shaded areas as well. With a band saw, cut along the outline for each of the cradle end pieces.

To cut out the hearts from the ends of the cradle, first drill a hole within each heart outline so you can insert the jigsaw blade. Then cut out the hearts with the jigsaw. Where indicated on the pattern, drill holes for the dowels using a 1-inch-diameter bit.

Bevel one long edge of each side piece and the two long sides of the bottom at a 14-degree angle. Glue and nail the sides to the bottom.

Dry fit the side-bottom unit by positioning it between the two cradle end pieces along the lines indicated on the pattern. Insert the dowels; check to see that they are flush with the ends of the cradle and that the side-bottom unit fits squarely against the ends. Make any necessary adjustments, then glue and nail all the pieces into place.

Countersink all nails and fill the holes with putty. Sand the edges and surfaces of the cradle until they're smooth. Paint the cradle with two coats of latex.

Enlarge the pattern for the flower motif, *below*, onto graph paper, flopping it along the center line. Using graphite paper and a sharp pencil, transfer the design to both ends of the cradle so that the design surrounds the heart cutouts.

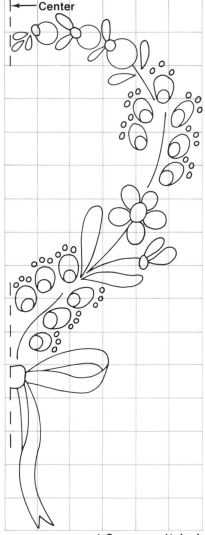

1 Square = ½ Inch

Referring to the photograph for guidance, paint one cluster of buds light blue with dark blue details and strokes of medium blue shading. Paint the other clusters pink, then add highlights in red and white.

Paint the leaves and stems green with dark green accents, and the daisies white with yellow centers and blue stamens. Add dots of yellow around the buds.

Finish the cradle with two coats of polyurethane.

Braided
♥ HEART RUG

Traditional braided rugs lend homespun warmth to any room in your house. This variation (below) of the classic oval rug is simple to shape when you bend the center strip at a 90-degree angle and work out from there.

Create your rug from dark, muted shades of woolen fabric or remnants, or change its personality completely by using light-color fabrics, plaids, or prints.

MATERIALS

Medium-weight, tightly woven, 100 percent wool fabrics *(See note, next page)*
Finger guards; darning needle
Heavy-duty lacing thread
C-clamp (wide enough to fit over table, plus about 1 inch to fit over braid)
3-inch T-pins

INSTRUCTIONS

Note: One square yard of fabric yields about 1 square foot of braided rug. The yardage required depends on the weight of the fabric and how tightly it is braided. Fifteen yards of fabric should be ample to make the rug.

The rug measures 30 inches from the top inside point to the bottom point, and 60 inches wide.

To cut fabric strips: Measure the fabric at 3-inch intervals along one edge. Make a small cut at each 3-inch mark, then tear the wool into long strips. (*Note:* For lighter weight fabrics, cut strips 4 inches wide.)

To piece the strips: Join the strips into 10- to 12-foot lengths by sewing them together along the bias (see drawing, *below*).

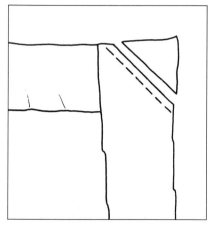

All the seams should be on the same side of the strip. Trim the seams and press them open.

Fold the strips in half lengthwise, then in half again. Fold them in half once more, so there are six layers of fabric, each about ½ inch wide.

Hold the folds in place by pinning them every 4 inches. Then roll each strip into a ball to store it until needed.

To braid the strips: Begin by unwrapping 4 feet from each of three balls. Stitch together two of the strips on the bias. Lay a third strip perpendicular to the two strips, forming a T. The third strip should begin at the seam of the first two strips. Slip-stitch the third strip in place.

Begin braiding the strips by bringing the left strip over the middle one, either by twisting or folding it over. Then bring the right strip over the middle strip, removing pins as you work.

After braiding 3 or 4 inches, secure the braid with a T-pin and use a C-clamp to attach the braided portion to a table or shelf.

Continue to braid, keeping an even tension on the strand between you and the clamp, and trying not to stretch it. A good braid is so tight that you cannot fit a pencil between the loops.

At the end of each 10- to 12-foot length, stitch new strips to the working strips and continue the braiding.

To create the heart shape: First, study the photograph to see how the rug is made. The braid begins in the center of the heart. From this point, the rug is assembled by working around and around the center braid, stitching adjoining braids together and shaping them into a heart as you go.

The braid running through the center of the heart should measure 36 inches. From the end of the braid, use T-pins to mark off a 36-inch length and the midpoint (18 inches) of the 36-inch length.

With the darning needle, insert lacing thread at the 36-inch mark. Bring the knotted end through the fold so the knot will be hidden.

Fold the braided strand at this point so that there are two rows of braids side by side. Begin lacing, catching the closest loop of the neighboring braid. (See the diagram, *below*.)

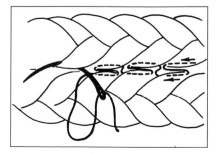

Work back and forth between the braids until they are secure. Keep the stitching taut, but not so tight as to keep the braids from lying flat.

Lace until you reach the midpoint of the 36-inch length. At this point, catch two loops on the outside braid for each one on the center braid. This is the beginning step in forming a V. When working on the inner 90-degree angle of the heart, the braid on which you pick up two loops will always be toward the top of the rug.

Note: It is only on the inner and outer curves that loops of the braid must be gathered two-for-one. On the straight sides, always loop one braid for one. To produce a flat rug, add symmetrically on both sides for even curves.

Continue lacing past that first inner curve. Then turn the outer curve by taking two loops on the inside of the curve for every one on the outside. Bend the braid back along the other side of the center braid.

When you reach the midpoint of the center braid again, take two loops on the center braid for one on the outside braid on either side of the midpoint.

Continue lacing, adding loops as needed on the outside curves and taking away as needed on the inside angle.

If you wish to change the braid colors and you want a symmetrical look, make the color changes at the same point every time. The best place to change is right before the curve where, laterally, there is an even number of braids from the center.

To finish the ends: When the rug reaches the desired size, or when you are at the end of a row, cut the braid about 6 inches past the finishing point.

Then cut the 6-inch strips lengthwise down the center, fold them in half, and slip-stitch the edges together.

With the lacing needle, pull each strip through a loop of the braid in the last row so that it blends in as much as possible with the rest of the rug. Pass each strip through several more loops for strength, then trim the ends close to the rug.

Hide the raw ends by tucking them under the last loop they were passed through. Secure the tucked ends with an invisible stitch whenever possible.

HEARTS
for the Holidays

♥ *With this chapterful of wreaths, candlesticks, greeting cards, and other holiday trims, you'll find it easy to spread the heartfelt joy of the season to family and friends.*

For Christmas giving or trimming the tree, stitch a few of the designs from the cupboard, opposite. Here are calico hearts to stitch and stuff, elegant ornaments bedecked with flowers and ribbons, and a pocket heart to fill with miniatures or candy.

Quilters will find a crazy-quilt heart to embroider, an ornament crafted from antique patchwork, and a heart worked in a feather wreath design using metallic thread.

Ornaments made of ribbons stitched or woven together and hearts to tat, crochet, and needlepoint complete the collection. Instructions begin on page 50.

GENERAL DIRECTIONS FOR FABRIC ORNAMENTS

For the fabric ornaments shown on page 49, follow these general directions:

Enlarge a basic heart shape, (such as a pattern on page 53) to the desired size and make a tissue paper pattern, adding ¼-inch seam allowances all around.

To add lace or piping, baste it to the right side of the heart front before assembling the ornament. Sew the front to the back with right sides facing; leave an opening for turning along one side of the heart.

Clip the curves at ⅛-inch intervals for smooth, rounded finished edges. Turn the heart right side out, stuff firmly, and slip-stitch closed. If desired, add a ribbon bow to the heart; tack a hanging loop to the back.

Sweet-and-Simple
♥ **CALICOES**

MATERIALS

Scraps of assorted calicoes
Assorted laces, ribbons, rickrack, and other trims
Polyester fiberfill

INSTRUCTIONS

The calico ornaments pictured on page 49 are about 3½ inches high. Follow the general directions for making a pattern. Cut two pieces from fabric. Stitch, turn, and stuff according to general directions. Embellish with trims, as desired.

Ribbon
♥ **STRIPS AND SQUARES**

MATERIALS

7-inch lengths of ½-inch-wide broadcloth ribbons
Fabric for ornament backs
Polyester fiberfill
Satin ribbon; lace trim
Gold beads

INSTRUCTIONS

Strip-pieced heart (shown in top row, second from left)

Lay lengths of ribbon side by side, overlapping edges slightly. Machine-zigzag-stitch the ribbons together.

Follow the general directions to make a 4½-inch-high ornament pattern. Position the pattern diagonally over the pieced ribbons and cut out the heart shape. Cut a fabric backing.

Add lace trim, then stitch and stuff the ornament according to general directions.

Woven ribbon heart (shown in third row, third from left)

Weave ribbons together to form a 7-inch square; baste around the edge. Follow general directions to make a 4½-inch-high pattern. Cut one heart from the woven square; cut a fabric backing.

Stitch and stuff the ornament according to general directions. At each point where the ribbons meet, stitch a gold bead.

Stitch-and-Stuff
♥ **POCKET**

MATERIALS

¼ yard of fabric
½ yard of lace
Polyester fiberfill
Miniature toys, dried flowers, candies, or other items

INSTRUCTIONS

This ornament is shown at the top right on page 49.

Follow the general directions to make a 5-inch-high heart pattern. Cut two hearts from fabric.

To make the pocket pattern, cut the heart pattern horizontally through the middle. Onto another sheet of paper, trace around the bottom half of the heart. Flop it along the upper edge, forming a diamond shape. Using this pattern, cut one piece from fabric.

Fold the fabric diamond in half (wrong sides together) along the line where you flopped the pattern. Press it, then baste it to the bottom of the ornament front, matching raw edges.

Follow the general directions for adding lace trim, stitching, and stuffing the heart. Fill the pocket with miniatures or other items, as desired.

Floral
♥ **NEEDLEPOINT HEART**

MATERIALS

8-inch square of No. 10-count needlepoint canvas
Yarn in colors listed in color key on page 10
¼ yard of print fabric
½ yard of ½-inch-wide lace
Polyester fiberfill

INSTRUCTIONS

Needlepoint the design following the chart on page 10. Cut the stitchery into the heart shape outlined on the chart, adding ½-inch seam margins. Cut a fabric backing the same size. Stitch and stuff the heart according to the general directions.

To make a ruffle, cut a 2½x40-inch rectangle from fabric. Fold it in half lengthwise. Sew along the raw edges, using a ¼-inch seam allowance, and leaving an opening for turning. Turn the ruffle right side out; press.

Gather the ruffle to fit around the heart; blindstitch it in place. Tack lace inside the ruffle.

Old-Fashioned
♥ **CRAZY QUILTING**

MATERIALS

Assorted fabrics
Scraps of embroidery floss
Embroidery hoop; needle
Beads or buttons
Polyester fiberfill

INSTRUCTIONS

This heart is pictured in the second row, second from right.

Make a 5-inch-high pattern for the heart according to the general directions. To make the ornament front, cut fabrics in small, irregular pieces. Stitch them together, right sides facing, until they form a piece of fabric that is as big as your pattern. Press seams to one side.

Embellish the heart front with a variety of embroidery stitches worked along the seam lines or within the patches. Cut the front from pieced fabric; cut a solid fabric backing.

Follow the general directions to stitch and stuff the ornament. Tack buttons or beads to the front.

Fanciful
♥ HEARTS WITH FLOWERS

MATERIALS
Assorted floral fabrics
Lace, ribbon, and braid trims
Small sprigs of flowers
Polyester fiberfill

INSTRUCTIONS
Follow the general directions to make a 3½-inch-high pattern. Cut a front and back from the fabric.

Stitch, stuff, and finish the heart according to the general directions. Embellish it with trims and flowers, referring to the photograph for ideas.

Antique
♥ PATCHWORK

MATERIALS
6-inch square of quilted fabric or portion of old, worn-out quilt
Piping; lace trim
Polyester fiberfill

INSTRUCTIONS
This ornament is shown at the bottom, second from left.

Follow the general directions to make a 4½-inch-high pattern. Cut the ornament front and back from quilted fabric.

Baste piping and lace to the ornament front; stitch and finish according to general directions.

Quilter's
♥ FEATHER WREATH

MATERIALS
¼ yard of white satin
Scrap of cotton fabric
Gold metallic thread
White lace trim
Polyester fiberfill

INSTRUCTIONS
Enlarge the pattern, *below*, onto graph paper, using a dark marking pen. With a water-erasable pen, trace the pattern onto the right side of the satin.

1 Square = ¹/₂ Inch

To stabilize the satin as you embroider, first baste cotton fabric behind the design. Using one strand of metallic thread, outline-stitch the design.

Cut out the heart ½ inch from the outer edge of the embroidered design; cut a matching piece from satin for the ornament back. Follow the general directions for stitching and stuffing the ornament, adding lace, if desired.

Quick-and-Easy
♥ CROCHETED HEART

MATERIALS
J. P. Coats Knit-Cro-Sheen
Size 8 steel crochet hook
White glue; ribbon

Gauge: 10 dc = 1 inch.

Abbreviations: See page 37.

INSTRUCTIONS
This ornament is shown in the bottom row, second from the right in the photograph on page 49. It measures 3 inches high.

Row 1: Ch 4; in 4th ch from hook work 4 dc; ch 3, turn.

Row 2: Work 3 dc in first dc, ch 1, sk dc, dc in next dc, ch 1, 3 dc in top of turning ch—2 ch-1 sps; ch 3, turn.

Row 3: Work 3 dc in first dc, ch 1, sk dc, dc in next dc, (dc in ch-1 sp, dc in dc) twice; ch 1, sk dc, 3 dc in next dc; ch 3, turn.

Row 4: Work 3 dc in first dc, ch 1, sk dc, dc in next dc, dc in ch-1 sp and * in each 5 dc *; dc in ch-1 sp and next dc; ch 1, sk dc, 3 dc in last dc; ch 3, turn.

Row 5: Work same as for Row 4, except bet *s work 9 dc.

Row 6: Work same as for Row 4, except bet *s work 13 dc.

Row 7: Work same as for Row 4, except bet *s work 17 dc.

Rows 8-9: Dc in 3 dc, ch 1, dc in next 21 dc, ch 1, dc in next 3 dc; ch 3, turn.

Row 10: Dc in 3 dc, ch 1, dc in next 9 dc, (ch 1, sk dc, dc in next dc) twice; dc in next 8 dc, ch 1, dc in 3 dc; ch 3, turn.

Top shaping: First rounded edge: Row 11: Sk first dc, dec over next 2 dc, dc in ch-1 sp, ch 1, sk dc, dc in 6 dc, ch 1, sk dc, dc in next dc; dec in next ch-1 sp and dc; ch 3, turn.

Row 12: Sk first dc, dec over next dc and ch-1 sp, dc in next dc, (ch 1, sk dc, dc in next dc) twice; ch 1, dc in ch-1 sp, dec over next 2 dc; ch 3, turn.

Row 13: Sk dc, dec over next dc and ch-1 sp, (dc in dc, dc in ch-1 sp) twice; dec over next 2 dc. Fasten off.

Second rounded edge: Row 11: Attach thread in center dc in Row 9; ch 3, dec over ch-1 sp and next dc, ch 1, sk dc, dc in 6 dc, ch 1, dc in ch-1 sp; dec over next 2 dc; ch 3 turn.

Rows 12-13: Work as for First Rounded Edge, ending Row 12 with dec over dc and top of ch-3. Fasten off.

Weave ⅛-inch-wide ribbon around the outer edge of the heart and tie it into a bow, if desired.

continued on page 52

Lacy
♥ TATTED TRIM

MATERIALS
One ball white DMC Cordonnet
 Special, Art. 151, Size 20
Two tatting shuttles
Size 12 steel crochet hook

INSTRUCTIONS
To begin, label the shs 1 and 2. To attach sh threads, unwind the specified length of thread from Sh 1, tie end with double knot to end of thread on Sh 2, and wind onto Sh 2, leaving 12 inches of thread free. Shs 1 and 2 are now joined.

After completing med, cut off excess thread at knot on Sh 2.

Inner med: Wind Sh 1 and leave 14 inches of thread free, to be used at WT. Wind Sh 2 half full. With Sh 1: *R 5 -- 5. T. With WT, ch 1-1. T*. Rep * - * 7 times. Cut both the sh thread and WT 3 inches from work; tie with a double knot to base of 1st R. Trim.

Rnd 2: Unwind 2½ yards of thread from Sh 1, tie to Sh 2 and wind onto Sh 2. Attach sh threads to any P of Rnd 1. With Sh 1 as AT and Sh 2 as WT, *ch 10. T. + (to next P of Rnd 1). T*. Rep * - * 6 times. Ch 10. T. + (to same P as 1st ch of Rnd 2). Do not cut threads.

Rnd 3: With Sh 2 as AT: *Ch 7-7. T. + (to next P of Rnd 1). T*. Rep * - * 6 times. Ch 7-7. T. + (to same P as 1st ch of Rnd 3). Do *not* cut threads.

Rnd 4: With Sh 1 as AT, *ch 9. With Sh 2, OR 4-4. Ch 9. T. + (to next P of Rnd 1). T. **Ch 9-9. T. + (to next P of Rnd 1). T**. Rep * - * 2 times. Rep ** - ** once. Ch 9-9. Cut both sh threads 3 inches from work; tie with a double knot to base of 1st ch of Rnd 4. Trim.

Bottom large med: Unwind 4 feet of thread from Sh 1, tie to Sh 2 and wind onto Sh 2. Sh 1: R 3-3-6. T. Ch 5+5 (to P of 2nd OR of Rnd 4). T. + (to 2nd P of PR). *R 3-3-6. T. Ch 5-5. T. + (to 2nd P of PR)*. Rep * - * once. R 3-3-6. T. Ch 5. Sh 2: JK 10. Ch 5. T. + (to 2nd P of PR). Rep * - * once. R 3-3+6 (to base of 1st R of med). T. Ch 5-5. Cut both sh threads 3 inches from

work; tie with a double knot to base of 1st R of med. Trim. Continue to work clockwise toward top.

(*) *First small med*: Unwind 2 feet of thread from Sh 1, tie to Sh 2 and wind onto Sh 2. Attach both sh threads between 1st and 2nd chs from bottom of previous large med. With Sh 1 as AT: Ch 7. Sh 2: JK 10. Ch 7. Sh 2: IR 2-2-2-2-2. T. With Sh 2 as AT: Ch 5+5 (to P of next ch of previous large med). T. + (to next P of PIR). T. *Ch 5-5. T. + (to next P of PIR). T*. Ch 5+5 (to P of next ch of inner med). T. + (to next P of PIR). T. Rep * - * once. Ch 5-5. Cut both sh threads 3 inches from work and tie with a double knot to base of PIR. Trim.

Second small med: Unwind 2 feet of thread from Sh 1, tie to Sh 2, wind onto Sh 2. Attach both sh threads between next two outer "petals" of previous small med. With Sh 1 as AT: Ch 7. Sh 2: JK 10. Ch 7. Sh 2: IR 2-2-2-2-2. T. *Ch 5+5 (to P of next ch of previous small med). T. + (to next P of PIR). T*. Rep * - * once. Ch 5+5 (to P of next OR of inner med). T. + (to next P of PIR). Rep * - * once. Ch 5-5. Cut both sh threads 3 inches from work and tie with a double knot to base of PIR. Trim.

Third small med: Unwind 2 feet of thread from Sh 1, tie to Sh 2; wind onto Sh 2. Attach both sh threads between next two outer "petals" of previous small med. With Sh 1 as AT: Ch 7. Sh 2: JK 10. Ch 7. Sh 2: IR 2-2-2-2-2. T. Ch 5+5 (to P of next "petal" of previous small med). T. + (to next P of PIR). T. Ch 5+5 (to P of same OR of inner med as previous small med). T. + (to next P of PIR). T. Rep * - * twice. Ch 5-5. Cut both threads 3 inches from work; double-knot to base of PIR. Trim.

Top large med: Unwind 4 feet of thread from Sh 1, tie to Sh 2 and wind onto Sh 2. Attach both sh threads between next two outer "petals" of previous small med. With Sh 1 as AT: Ch 7. Sh 2: JK 10. Ch 7. Sh 2: R 3-3-6. T. With Sh 2 as AT: Ch 5+5 (to P of next "petal" of previous small med). T. + (to 2nd P of PR). *R 3-3-6. T. Ch 5-5. T. + (to 2nd P of PR)*. Rep * -

* twice. R 3-3-6. T. Ch 5. Sh 1: JK 10. Ch 5. T. + (to 2nd P of PR). R 3-3+6 (to base of 1st R of med). T. Ch 5-5. Cut both sh threads 3 inches from work; tie with a double knot to base of 1st R of med. Trim.

Fourth small med: Unwind 2 feet of thread from Sh 1, tie to Sh 2 and wind onto Sh 2. Attach both sh threads between next two chs of previous large med to the right of JK. With Sh 1 as AT: Ch 7. Sh 2: JK 10. Ch 7. Sh 2: IR 2-2-2-2-2. T. Ch 5+5 (to P of next ch of previous large med). T. + (to next P of PIR). T. Rep * - * 3 times. Ch 5-5. Cut both sh threads 3 inches from work; tie with a double knot to base of PIR. Trim (*). Turn work around and rep (*) - (*) once to complete other side of heart.

Unwind 18 inches of thread from Sh 1, tie to Sh 2; wind onto Sh 2. Attach threads between 2nd and 3rd outer "petals" of 4th small med. Ch 7. T. + (to P of top ch of inner med). T. Ch 7. Cut both sh threads 3 inches from work; tie with a double knot between 2nd and 3rd outer "petals" of right top small med. Trim.

TATTING ABBREVIATIONS

AT	anchor thread
ch	chain
IR	inner ring
JK	Josephine knot
med	medallion
OR	outer ring
P(s)	picot(s)
PIR	previous inner ring
PR	previous ring
R	ring
rep	repeat
rnd	round
sh	shuttle
T	turn
WT	working thread
+	join to picot as indicated in ( )
-	picot, leave a space of $^{3}/_{16}$ inch between double knots for a picot
--	large picot, leave a space of ½ inch between double knots for a ¼-inch picot

Papier-Mâché
♥ **CHRISTMAS TRIMS**

A few pieces of cardboard and bits of newspaper, paste, and paint are all you need to create a houseful of these cheerful papier-mâché Christmas tree and door ornaments. Simple enough for children to make, the trims are a delightful preholiday project for the entire family.

MATERIALS
Lightweight cardboard
White glue; flour
Newspaper; brown paper
Thin cotton string or fine crochet thread
White, red, and green acrylic paints; gold metallic paint
High-gloss plastic glaze
Paper clips
Graph paper; graphite paper
Ribbon
Black felt-tip marker
Fine-tip paintbrushes

INSTRUCTIONS
Enlarge the patterns, *right*, onto graph paper. These will be your master patterns. Transfer the outlines to cardboard; cut out the heart shapes. Place a paper clip on each ornament so that it extends ¼ inch from the center top.

To make the papier-mâché paste, cook 2 cups of water and 6 tablespoons of flour until thickened. When cool, mix with 3 tablespoons of white glue. (*Note:* If covered and refrigerated, the paste will keep for several days.)

Cut newspaper and brown paper into ¼-inch-wide strips. Dip the newspaper strips into the paste, then lay them across each cardboard shape. Smooth them with your fingers, rounding the edges and covering the paper clip to secure it to the cardboard.

When you have covered the shapes with newspaper strips, repeat with the brown paper strips until the ornaments are about ¼

inch thick. Trim the excess paper from around the edges and smooth the ends of the paper strips into place.

When dry, paint each ornament with two coats of white acrylic. Let the paint dry thoroughly, then transfer the design details to

1 Square = 1 Inch

both sides of each ornament using graphite paper.

Using white glue, secure cotton string or thread around the edges of each ornament (a toothpick helps to push the thread into place). Also glue thread around the edge of each flower, berry, and

leaf. Repeat the process for the other side of each ornament.

Paint the designs on the ornaments with red and green acrylics, referring to the photograph for color combinations. Let dry. With a fine-tip brush, paint the cotton thread gold. Repeat for both sides of each ornament.

When the paint is completely dry, use a black marker to make an X in each berry for a stem. Lacquer the ornaments with a coat of high-gloss plastic glaze; let them dry thoroughly.

To finish, thread a length of ribbon through the paper clip loop at the top; hang in place.

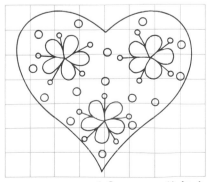

1 Square = ½ Inch

Pretty Paper
♥ CARDS AND
BASKETS

By experimenting with a
variety of craft papers, you
can fold and cut these
"snowflake" cards for
holiday greetings, or create
an array of baskets and
cornucopias to use as tree
trims and party favors.

MATERIALS
Note cards
Sturdy paper for cards
Tissue or other lightweight paper
  for cutout designs
White glue or rubber cement
Clear adhesive-backed vinyl
Artist's brayer
Baskets and cornucopias
Sturdy paper in at least two colors
White glue or rubber cement

INSTRUCTIONS
General instructions: All the projects shown may be made from a
variety of papers. Referring to the
information, *opposite,* choose the
paper according to its strength
and workability.

For all the projects, use either
rubber cement or white glue. Rubber cement will dry quickly into a
thin, transparent film, and any
excess can be rubbed away with
your finger. White glue is strong
but should be used in small dots so
it won't soak through the paper.

Use a large pair of scissors for
straight cuts and large shapes,
and a smaller pair for more intri-
cate cutting.

To preserve the paper projects,
seal them with clear adhesive-
backed vinyl as explained for the
note cards, *right,* or use other
clear sealing products.

Coat flat surfaces with several
coats of clear acrylic spray or

acrylic medium (available in art
stores) applied with a soft brush.
This will protect projects that are
not subjected to constant han-
dling. For other paper-covered
surfaces, brush on up to 20 coats
of plastic glaze (available in crafts
stores) for strong, durable protection. The glaze is a white, milky
liquid that dries strong and clear.

For maximum protection when
paper projects are not in use, store
them away from excessive heat,
moisture, and direct sunlight.
Note cards
For each card, cut sturdy paper
into a rectangle that measures either 4x8 inches or 5x10 inches.
Fold it in half to make the card.
Cut tissue (or other paper) into a
square the same size as the front
of the note card.

Referring to the diagram at the
top of the page, *opposite,* fold the
paper in half, and in half again to
form a smaller square. Fold the

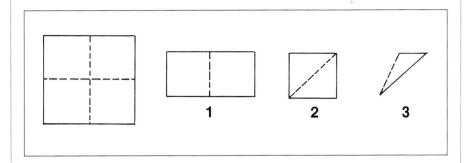

square in half diagonally, keeping all folded edges together.

Using small, sharp scissors, cut designs into the folded paper as you would for paper snowflakes. Experiment with a variety of shapes, working hearts into the designs. If you like, practice on scrap paper, drawing the cutting lines on the paper before you cut. Make copies of favorite designs.

Center the tissue cutout on the front of the note card and secure it in place with *small* amounts of rubber cement or glue.

To protect the card, cut a piece of adhesive vinyl and affix it to the front and back of the note card; roll firmly and evenly with an artist's brayer to remove air bubbles. Trim the excess vinyl.

Heart baskets

For each basket, cut two 2x6-inch rectangles—one red and one white. Fold each in half crosswise and round the corners opposite the fold. In each piece, make two 2-inch-deep cuts, starting at the fold. (See Diagram 1, *right*.)

As you assemble the basket, slip folded strips around or through each other, not over and under each other. (See Diagram 2.)

Holding the folds away from you, slip the first strip of the red piece (A) through the first strip of the white piece (B). Then slip the middle strip around the corresponding middle strip, and so forth. (See Diagram 3.)

Take the second strip of A and slip it around the first strip of B, through the second, and around the third strip. (See Diagram 4.) Repeat the first step for the remaining strips.

Cut a ¼x6-inch paper strip for the handle. Glue the ends to the inside of the basket.

To vary the baskets, adjust the sizes and proportions of the paper pieces and the width of the strips.

Paper cornucopias

For each cornucopia, cut a 10-inch-diameter circle from paper. Cut the circle in half and overlap the straight edges to form a cone; glue edges together. Cut a heart from a contrasting-color paper. Glue the heart to the front; add a strip of paper for the handle.

CHOOSING CRAFT PAPER

Here are qualities to look for as you buy papers for craft projects.

Art papers are high-quality, usually expensive papers designed for pen and ink, watercolors, pastels, or other "fine arts." They often have exciting textural qualities that lend interest to collages and handcrafted cards.

All-purpose papers include typing paper, manila drawing paper, and dime store tablets. Use them for roughing out ideas.

Kraft paper is a generic term for brown wrapping paper, usually sold in rolls, that is popular for packaging and pattern making.

Newsprint is an inexpensive paper available in large pads. Though flimsy, its large size and low cost make it useful for sketching and children's crafts.

Construction paper is a multipurpose paper available in many colors. It is usually sold in packages of sheets with a matte finish.

Crepe paper is available in rolls or sheets in many festive colors. Though lightweight and not especially durable, it does withstand pulling, rolling, and twisting.

Tissue paper is fragile, but it is lightweight, transparent, and available in several shades.

Origami paper is light- to medium-weight, usually sold in 2- to 10-inch-square sheets in brilliant colors, prints, and foils. Although thin, it is sturdy and creases well, making a lighter weight alternative to construction paper for collages and cards.

Gift wraps come in a wide range of colors and finishes, often printed with motifs that can be used individually in other projects.

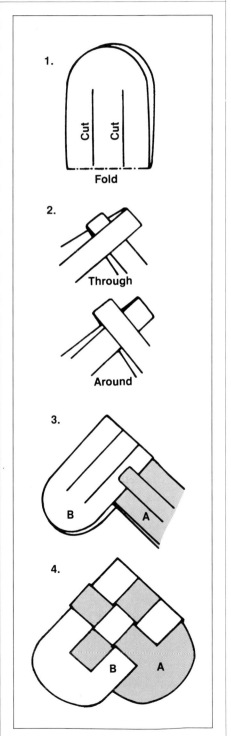

Cross-Stitched
♥CRAZY-QUILT STOCKING

Like an old-fashioned crazy quilt, this stocking is a charming patchwork of cross-stitched "blocks" filled with hearts and Christmas motifs. The 8x13-inch stocking is worked on 22-count hardanger fabric. But by using an even-weave fabric with fewer threads to the inch, you can make the stocking larger, if desired.

MATERIALS
22x24 inches of ecru hardanger fabric
Embroidery floss in the colors listed in the color key, page 58
1 yard of teal cotton fabric
1 yard of ¼-inch-diameter cotton cable cord
16 inches of ½-inch-wide lace trim
¼ yard of polyester fleece
Gold glass beads
Embroidery hoop

INSTRUCTIONS
As shown on the chart on pages 58-59, the stocking front and cuff are separate cross-stitched pieces. To fit both pieces on the hardanger, stitch the stocking front vertically on the length of the fabric. Turn the cuff on its side and work it next to the stocking.

Tape or zigzag-stitch the edges of the hardanger to prevent them from raveling as you work. As you stitch, use two strands of floss and work over two threads of fabric. Always work the cross-stitches in the same direction.

To begin, use a waste knot to anchor the thread end in the fabric. Following the chart and color key on pages 58-59, begin stitching the toe of the stocking in the lower left-hand corner of the hardanger, leaving at least a 3-inch margin of fabric beyond the cross-stitched outline of the stocking.

Work the entire outline of the stocking. Then work the outline of the cuff, leaving at least 1½ inches between the right-hand top of the stocking and the cuff.

When you have completed the outlines, fill in the stocking front and cuff. In some areas of the chart, large blocks of solid color are represented by a single symbol. Work these areas in the color indicated, referring to the photograph for guidance.

When you have finished stitching, press the fabric gently on the wrong side.

To assemble the stocking, cut out the cross-stitched stocking front ½ inch beyond the outline. Cut out the cuff, leaving ½ inch along the bottom and sides and 3 inches beyond the top outline.

From teal fabric, cut three pieces the same size as the stocking front (for the backing and lining), one piece to match the cuff, and enough bias strips to cover the cable cord. From fleece, cut one piece the same size as the stocking front and another 3¼x8-inch piece.

Piece together the bias fabric strips and use a zipper foot to stitch them over the cable cord. Pin the cord to the stocking front, positioning it just inside the cross-stitched outline. Baste it in place.

Baste the fleece to the wrong side of the stocking front. At this point, stitch glass beads to the front of the stocking, referring to the photograph for placement.

With right sides facing, stitch the stocking front to the back, using a ½-inch seam allowance and sewing as close to the cable cord as possible. Leave the top of the stocking open. Grade the seam and clip the curves.

To line the stocking, stitch the two lining pieces together, right sides facing. Leave the top open. Trim the seam; clip curves. With wrong sides facing, slip the lining over the stocking. Stitch the top edges together using a ½-inch seam allowance. Pull the stocking out and slip the lining inside.

To finish the cuff, baste the fleece to the wrong side of the cross-stitched portion of the cuff front. Stitch the front to the teal piece along both short ends, right sides facing; trim seams. Press under ½ inch along each raw edge of the cuff. Then fold the cuff in half, matching the pressed edges. Blindstitch the edges together.

Slip the cuff over the top of the stocking so the bottom of the cuff conceals the top inch of the stocking. Slip-stitch the top of the stocking to the inside of the cuff.

Tack lace to the cuff bottom.

CROSS-STITCH TECHNIQUES
To help perfect your cross-stitched projects, follow these tips as you work.

Embroidery hoops can leave marks on the fabric and, if left on the fabric for a long time, can distort the material permanently. Wrap the hoop with tissue paper to prevent it from marking the fabric. And be sure to remove the fabric from the hoop whenever you stop stitching, even if for only a short time.

When stitching a project with many small motifs, avoid continually starting and stopping your thread by carrying the floss across the back of the fabric. To carry the floss, slip the threaded needle under previous stitches. Do not carry a thread loosely to another area, because a too-tight tension will make the fabric pucker. If the tension is too loose, the back will become messy and cause threads to tangle and twist.

To help ensure that you count the stitches correctly, work the outline or border of the design first, continually double-checking the placement of the stitches. Then, fill in the work. This will prevent ripping out stitches, which will ruin the look of a work if you are using dark threads that can leave stains on light fabric.

When you have completed the stitching, finish the work with a thorough pressing. Lay a thick towel over an ironing board and place the stitchery right side down over the towel. Dampen a press cloth and lay it atop the stitchery. Then press the piece using a moderately hot iron.

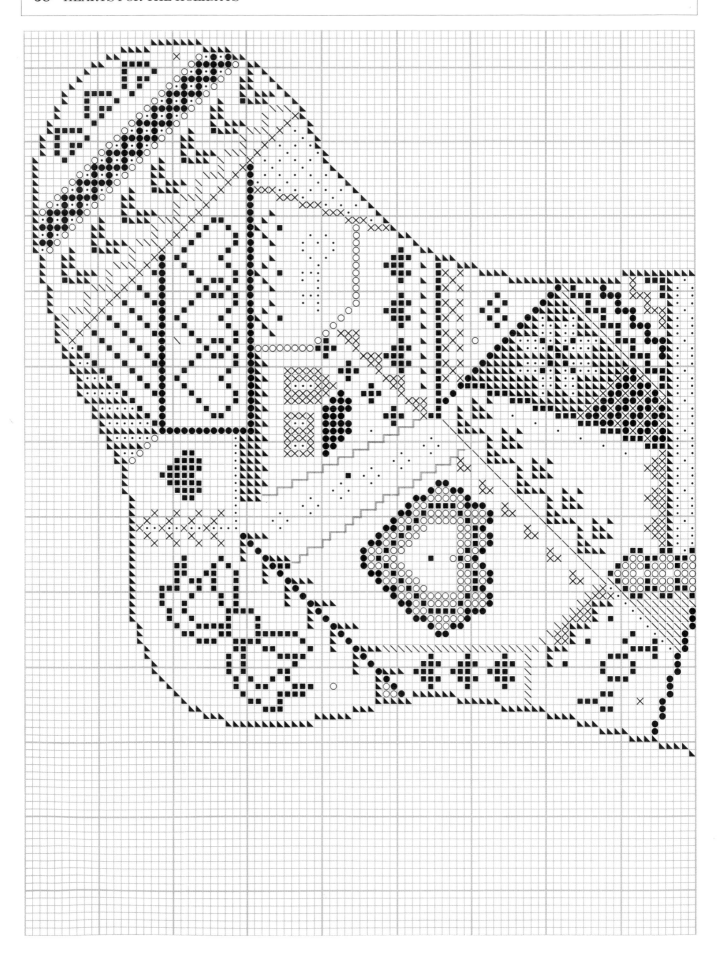

COLOR KEY
◣ Dark Olive Green
■ Brick Red
○ Coral
· Mustard Yellow
✕ Teal
● Auburn
◹ Light Brown

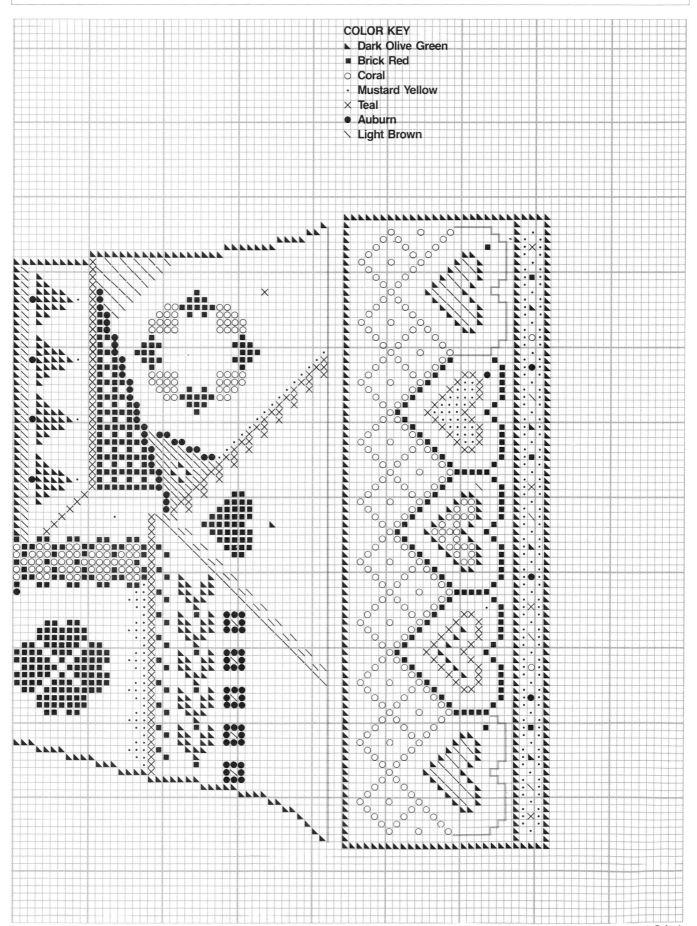

1 Square = 1 Stitch

Old-World
♥ **WREATH TO EMBROIDER**

A graceful adaptation of the classic heart shape was the inspiration for this masterpiece of satin and stem stitches. Its bright-colored flosses and bold design make it a refreshing wreath for Christmas or a colorful mirror frame to use throughout the year.

MATERIALS
1 yard of muslin
Three skeins of embroidery floss in each of the colors listed in the color key, *below*
Fifteen 5-mm gold beads
Fifty-four 3-mm gold beads
3 yards of gold cording
1 yard of thick quilt batting
18-inch square of foam-core board
12-inch square of mirror tile
Glass cutter
White glue
Masking tape
Water-erasable transfer pen
Graph paper

INSTRUCTIONS
Enlarge the pattern, *below*, onto graph paper. From muslin, cut two 22x26-inch pieces; set one piece aside.

Tape the other piece to a window and slip the pattern behind it, positioning the pattern so that there is at least ¾ inch of fabric beyond the solid outlines on the pattern. With water-erasable pen, trace the design onto the muslin.

Stretch the muslin in an embroidery hoop. Work stems in medium green, using a stem stitch and six strands of floss. Work remaining areas in satin stitches with three strands, referring to the color key, *below*. Stitch leaves in shades of green and the unnumbered flower centers in yellow. Outline a few of the flower centers with stem stitches.

When the stitchery is completed, gently rinse it in cold water to remove the pen marks. When dry, press the stitchery on the wrong side, using a press cloth.

Stitch a large gold bead over each X indicated on the pattern, and a smaller bead on each circle.

Adding ¾-inch seam margins to the inner and outer edges of the heart, cut out the heart shape.

From the remaining muslin, cut a matching piece for the backing.

Using the graph paper pattern as a guide, cut the wreath shape from foam-core board. Cut two layers of quilt batting the same size as the board; glue the batting to one side of the board.

Stretch the embroidery over the batting and board; tape and glue the raw edges to the back. To conceal the raw edges, turn under ¾ inch along the edges of the muslin backing; whipstitch it to the wreath back.

Slip-stitch gold cording to the inner and outer edges of the wreath, overlapping the ends at the bottom and stitching them to the back of the wreath.

To add a mirror to the wreath, use a glass cutter to trim a mirror tile to 10½x11 inches. Trim the corners so they don't extend beyond the edges of the wreath.

Secure the mirror in place by cutting a piece of muslin slightly larger than the mirror. Turn under the raw edges, lay the fabric over the back of the mirror, and securely stitch the edges of the fabric to the back of the wreath, encasing the mirror. Add a wire loop for hanging.

COLOR KEY

1. Light Red	3. Lavender	5. Magenta	7. Light Turquoise
2. Medium Red	4. Purple	6. Gold	8. Medium Turquoise

1 Square = 1 Inch

Country-Style
♥ **WREATH AND CANDLESTICKS**

Turn a traditional evergreen wreath into an extra-special greeting by shaping it into a classic heart. Simple enough to make on Christmas Eve, this wreath begins as a wire coat hanger and evergreen branches; in just a few minutes it becomes a door or window decoration that extends a heart-warming hello.

For your holiday table, the romance of candlelight is enhanced by these heart-shape candlesticks. They're perfect for gifts or a Christmas Eve vigil—but don't pack them away after the holidays are over. They also make delightful accessories for Valentine's Day or for decorating all year long.

MATERIALS
Wreath
About five pounds of greens (such as white or Scotch pine)
Wire coat hanger
Light-gauge wire
Wire clippers
Candlesticks
1¼-inch-thick pine
½-inch-thick pine
Jigsaw or coping saw
Drill with ¼- and ¾-inch bits
¼-inch-diameter doweling
Sandpaper
Wood glue
Red enamel paint

INSTRUCTIONS
Wreath
Bend a coat hanger into a heart shape, pulling the bottom and center top down. Clip off the hook at the top of the hanger.

Beginning at one curve of the heart shape and working toward the bottom point, wrap branches of greens tightly around the coat hanger and secure them in place with light-gauge wire. Repeat for the other side, beginning at the curve and working down.

Then, beginning at the curves again, work over the curves and toward the top inside point of the heart, wrapping the branches tightly as you go.

When the entire coat hanger is concealed with branches, clip the remaining greens into short pieces and work them between the wire to attach them to the heart as desired. Continue adding greens until the heart is full and well shaped.

If desired, decorate the wreath with wooden or fabric heart ornaments, clusters of dried flowers, ribbon bows or streamers, or other trims.

Candlesticks
As shown in the photograph, the candlesticks can be made in various sizes. To make a 4¾-inch-high candlestick, draw a 4¾-inch square on 1¼-inch-thick pine.

Draw a heart shape inside the square so that the center top and bottom points of the heart are centered on opposite sides of the square, and so the heart extends to the square's edges. Cut out the square.

On the edges of the block, mark the center top and bottom points of the heart. Drill a ¾-inch-diameter hole 2 inches deep into the center top for the candle.

Drill a ¼-inch-diameter hole ½ inch deep into the center bottom of the block. This hole will be used to fasten the candlestick to its base.

With a jigsaw or coping saw, cut out the heart. Sand until smooth.

To make a base for the heart, cut a 1x2-inch piece from ½-inch-thick pine. Bevel the edges slightly as shown in the photograph.

To attach the heart to the stand, drill a ¼-inch-diameter hole through the center of the base. Put a drop of glue into the hole in the bottom of the candlestick, then insert a 1-inch length of dowel to connect the base to the heart. Let the glue dry, then paint the candlestick as desired.

To vary the size of the candlesticks, begin with a 3½-inch or 5-inch square, as desired.

HEARTFELT
Sayings

♥ *Designed around classic and endearing sayings, the projects in this chapter are expressions not just of your crafting skills, but of your feelings, too. Whether you make a needlepoint friendship sampler or huggable bunny toy, a homey cross-stitched pillow or a folk-art painted welcome sign, the finished product will reflect your heartfelt sentiments.*

Romance is unmistakable in the lilac wreath shown here. By using the same cross-stitched lilac motifs, you can create elegant decorating accessories such as the pillowcases, opposite. For instructions, please turn the page.

"Your Love for Mine"
♥ **LILAC WREATH**

shown on page 65

MATERIALS

At least 26x28 inches of lavender, white, or ecru hardanger fabric

Embroidery floss in the colors listed in the color key, *page 68*

Embroidery hoop or artist's stretcher bars

INSTRUCTIONS

Determining the amount of fabric required: The lilac wreath design shown on page 65 is worked on a 26x28-inch piece of hardanger, then framed, leaving a ½-inch margin of fabric beyond the outermost points of the stitching.

To determine the amount of fabric to buy, first decide how you wish to frame the finished stitchery and the dimensions of the backing over which the stitchery will be stretched.

When worked over two threads of hardanger, the finished stitchery will measure 12½ inches from top to bottom and 15½ inches wide. Add extra inches to these measurements if you wish to surround the stitchery with a plain border of fabric.

Also, since the stretched stitchery sets *inside* the frame, it will be covered in the front by the width of the frame. Add extra length and width to your dimensions for this overlap.

Finally, before determining the finished size of the stretched fabric, add 1 inch on each side for folding the fabric around the edges of the backing.

To begin stitching: Locate the center of your hardanger and the center of the chart on pages 68-69. On the chart, every tenth grid square is marked with a heavy line. Graph these lines on the fabric by basting a row of stitches every 20 threads (stitches will be worked over two threads). As you cross-stitch and count the stitches, match the fabric grid to the heavy lines on the chart.

Bind the edges of the fabric with masking tape to prevent raveling. Stretch the fabric in an embroidery hoop or artist's stretcher strips and begin stitching, using three strands of floss and working over two threads of fabric.

To avoid knots on the back of the fabric, thread floss and knot one end. Insert the needle into the right side of the fabric about 6 inches away from the placement of the first cross-stitch.

Work the cross-stitches; when finished, clip the waste knot. Rethread the needle with the six inches of excess floss and weave the floss through the backs of the stitches.

Note: See page 56 for more information on cross-stitch.

Follow the color key on page 68 to work the design. Complete the leaves before stitching the lilacs.

Each lilac is outlined on the chart. Within each outline are symbols for stitches worked in dark purple and gray-blue. Work these stitches first. Then, around each gray-blue stitch, work four light lavender cross-stitches. Work the rest of the outlined area in light purple.

Flop the pattern along the center line to complete the left half, referring to the basted lines on the fabric for guidance.

When you have completed the wreath, work the saying, positioning it as indicated by the letter L within the wreath chart.

After completing the stitchery, press the hardanger on the wrong side, using a press cloth and a medium-hot iron. Frame according to the directions, *right*, or take the stitchery to a professional framer.

If desired, you can sew the cross-stitched wreath into a pillow instead of framing it. Draw an outline of the pillow front on the hardanger, leaving at least a 1-inch margin outside the outermost cross-stitches.

Cut out the pillow front and a matching fabric backing. Add lace to the pillow front, if desired. Stitch the front to back, right sides together, leaving an opening. Turn the pillow right side out, stuff it, and blindstitch it closed.

FRAMING EMBROIDERIES

With the following tips, you can finish your stitchery with the professional look of framing.

Determine the finished size of the stretched stitchery according to the instructions, *left*. Subtract ⅛ inch all around from the measurements to determine the dimensions of the batting and backing you will use, and of the *back* opening in the frame.

Purchasing the frame: If you plan to buy an assembled frame, take a tape measure with you to measure the opening on the *back* of the frame. You also can have frames cut to size at a framing shop and assemble them yourself.

Preparation: Draw the length and width of the backing (determined above) onto foam-core board or heavy cardboard. Cut out; cut batting to match.

Clean the stitchery if necessary and *press it thoroughly*, using a press cloth.

Mark the desired dimensions of the stretched stitchery onto the fabric. Baste along these lines; the basting threads will serve as a guide when stretching the piece.

Locate the center of the width and length of the stitchery on all four sides and snip the fabric to mark these points. Mark corresponding points on the backing.

Assembly: Tape or staple the batting to the backing. Center the stitchery atop the batting, matching the notches on the fabric to the marks on the backing.

Pull the excess fabric tautly over the edges of the backing from top to bottom, side to side, and from opposite corners. Tape or staple the fabric to the back. Each time you pull, check the stitchery front to see that the grain of the fabric is straight.

Framing: Place the stretched stitchery into the frame; secure with framing tacks. Cover the back with brown paper; add a wire loop for hanging. (*Note:* Avoid using glass in frames. Glass traps air, creating condensation that can cause fabric discoloration and deterioration.)

Lilac
♥PILLOWCASE BORDER
shown on page 65

MATERIALS
Set of purchased pillowcases
  or 2 to 2½ yards of lavender
  or white cotton fabric to
  make your own (see note on
  measurements, *below*)
One 4½x41-inch strip of
  lavender or white hardanger
  fabric
Embroidery floss in the colors
  listed in the color key, *page 68*
1¼ yards of purple piping
1¼ yards of crocheted or
  purchased lace
Embroidery hoop, needle

INSTRUCTIONS
Note: Ready-made pillowcases are available in standard, queen, and king sizes. Standard pillowcases measure 20x30 inches; queen-size, 20x34 inches; and king-size, 20x40 inches.

If you plan to make your pillowcases, buy 44-inch-wide cotton fabric as follows: 2 yards for standard, 2¼ yards for queen size, and 2½ yards for king size. This is sufficient for two pillowcases.

Because the width is the same for all pillowcases, the cross-stitched border band will be the same length no matter which pillowcase size you use.

To begin stitching: Locate the center of the single lilac motif, *right,* and the center of the 4½x41-inch strip of hardanger. Beginning at this point on the fabric, work the cross-stitch design following the chart, *right,* and color key, *page 68.*

Space the motifs evenly along the strip and center them between the two long edges. You can work six repeats to cover just half the strip, or work enough to go all the way around.

Assembling the pillowcases: For each pillowcase, cut a piece of lavender or white cotton fabric so it is the length of the finished pillowcase (30, 34, or 40 inches) plus 5 inches, and 41 inches wide.

Fold the fabric in half, right sides together, so it is 20½ inches wide. Stitch along one end and the long edge. Trim the seams and finish the raw edges with zigzag stitches.

Turn ¼ inch along the open edge of the pillowcase to the *right* side. Press and baste.

Using a zipper foot, stitch piping to the right side of the pillowcase so the cording is just beyond the edge of the fabric. With the pillowcase turned right side out, turn up a 3-inch-wide cuff. Baste it into place.

Fold under the long edges of the cross-stitched lilac band so it is 3 inches wide; turn under ½ inch on each short end.

Pin the band over the pillowcase cuff, positioning it so that the top edge is next to the piping and the ends of the band meet on the center back of the pillowcase. Baste into place.

With lavender thread, topstitch the band to the pillowcase cuff, stitching as close to the edges as possible. Blindstitch the overlapping ends together.

If desired, trim the finished pillowcases with crocheted or purchased lace blindstitched to the edge of the cross-stitched band. (*Note:* Instructions for the crocheted lace shown on page 65 appear on page 39.)

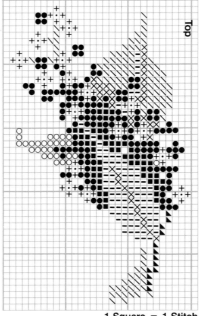

1 Square = 1 Stitch

CROSS-STITCHING WITH WASTE CANVAS
Although cross-stitch instructions often specify a certain type of fabric, you can substitute almost any material when you use waste canvas, a special cotton "grid" designed for working counted cross-stitch on fabrics other than hardanger, Aida cloth, and other even-weaves.

The finished look of stitchery worked with waste canvas is identical to that of counted thread work; however, the background fabric may be batiste, broadcloth, gabardine, poplin, wool, or a variety of other fabrics. This process offers more options when choosing background fabrics for counted thread work.

Waste canvas comes in 10 and 14 squares to the inch. It is a mono canvas rather than an interlock or penelope canvas. (*Note:* If you are substituting a different fabric for the material specified in the instructions, count the number of stitches you'll get to the inch using the waste canvas and adjust the yardage and placement of the stitches accordingly.)

Buy enough waste canvas so you won't have to piece it; piecing can produce cross-stitches that are not uniform in size or shape.

Lay the waste canvas atop the background fabric so the grid of the canvas is even with the grain of the fabric, and so a square of the canvas is centered over the *center* of the fabric. Pin the canvas in place, then sew it to the fabric using long basting stitches.

Begin cross-stitching from the center square. To work a cross-stitch, insert the threaded needle through the smallest spaces on the canvas. Avoid catching any of the canvas in the stitches, or it will be difficult to remove the canvas threads later and you may distort some of the stitches.

When all the stitching is complete, remove the basting threads. Then moisten the canvas thoroughly and gently pull out the canvas threads one at a time until all are removed.

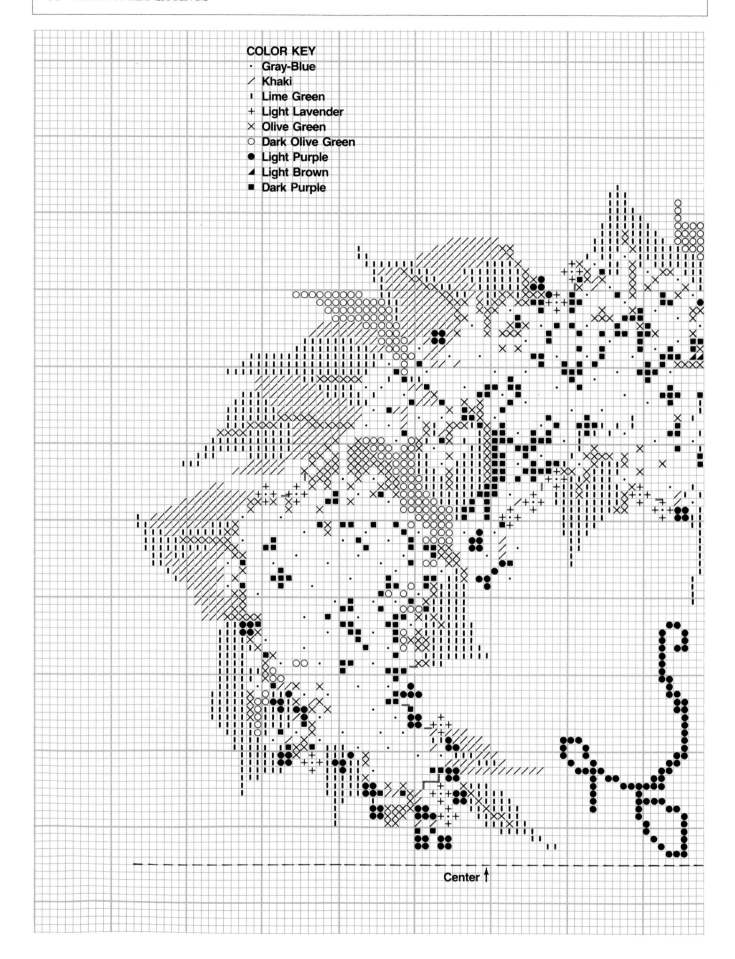

COLOR KEY
· Gray-Blue
/ Khaki
I Lime Green
+ Light Lavender
× Olive Green
○ Dark Olive Green
● Light Purple
◤ Light Brown
■ Dark Purple

Center ↑

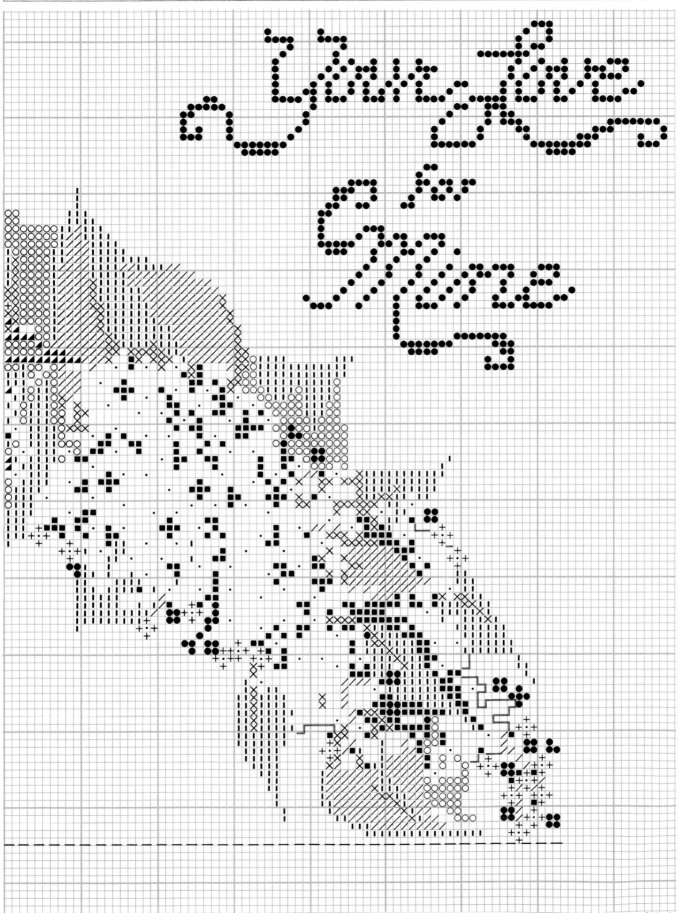

1 Square = 1 Stitch

"Home Is Where the Heart Is"
♥ **PILLOW TO CROSS-STITCH**

Long a favorite sentiment in cross-stitched samplers, this classic home-and-heart saying is perfect for a pillow edged with ruffles of fabric and lace.

MATERIALS
One 20-inch square of white hardanger fabric
1 yard of fabric for pillow backing and ruffle
1 yard of 1-inch-wide pregathered lace
Embroidery floss in colors listed in color key, *opposite*
Embroidery hoop; tapestry needle
Masking tape
Polyester fiberfill
1 yard of cotton cording

INSTRUCTIONS
Note: See the tip boxes on pages 56 and 67 for information on cross-stitch techniques.

Before you begin stitching, bind the raw edges of the hardanger with masking tape to prevent raveling while you work.

Beginning 4 inches from the bottom center of the hardanger, stitch the outline of the heart shape, starting with the bottom point of the heart. Using three

strands of floss, work each stitch in the same direction over two threads of fabric. Weave the ends of the strands of floss under previously worked stitches.

When you have completed the outline, cross-stitch the saying, flowers, and hearts within the heart shape.

Wash the completed stitchery, if desired, then lightly steampress it on the wrong side using a press cloth.

To assemble the pillow, trim the pillow front 1 inch beyond the cross-stitched heart outline. Cut a piece of backing fabric to the same size as the pillow front.

Also from backing fabric, cut enough pieces to make a 5x100-inch strip for the ruffle and enough bias strips to cover the cotton cording. To make the ruffle, fold the 5x100-inch strip in half lengthwise, wrong sides together, and sew two rows of gathering

stitches along the raw edge. Gather the ruffle to fit the pillow front.

Baste the covered cording, pregathered lace, and ruffle to the right side of the pillow front.

With right sides together, stitch the front to the back, using a ½-inch seam margin, and checking to see that the ruffles are not caught in the stitching. Leave an opening for turning.

Turn the pillow right side out, stuff, and slip-stitch closed.

COLOR KEY
◪ Celery
▯ Olive
◙ Pale Pink
◖ Coral
◤ Rose

1 Square = 1 Stitch

"Willkommen"
♥ PAINTED SIGN

Beautifully painted and colorful signs are a hallmark of Old World country hospitality. What nicer way to greet your own visitors than with this welcoming heart, adapted from a traditional design.

The heart bears a subtly shaded wreath of flowers painted with acrylics, coated with an antique finish, and buffed with turpentine for a weathered look. Even if you're unfamiliar with decorative painting techniques, you'll find this project a snap to make.

The heart measures 15x17 inches.

MATERIALS

Wooden heart (available at craft and hobby stores) or ½-inch-thick plywood to make your own
Red and white base paints
Green, yellow, blue, red, brown, and white acrylic paints
Fine-tip paintbrush
Antiquing stain
Varnish
Turpentine
Sandpaper
Graph paper; graphite paper

INSTRUCTIONS

Purchase a wooden heart or cut a 15x17-inch heart shape from ½-inch-thick plywood. Sand the edges and surfaces smooth.

Paint the heart with red base paint and allow it to dry thoroughly. (*Note:* Always let paint dry completely before adding another coat. Paint as many areas of one color at a time as possible.)

With pencil, sketch a heart outline 2 inches inside the edge of the wooden heart. Paint this inset white, using two or three coats.

Enlarge the pattern, *right*, onto graph paper. Lay graphite paper atop the wooden heart and center the pattern over it. Trace the design to transfer it to the wood.

The pattern shows the outlines of the motifs. As you paint, add details with darker or lighter colors, referring to the photograph for placement.

Experiment with mixing paint colors for hues different from those shown here. You can create a soft, weathered effect by diluting the paint with water and applying a light wash of color. Highlight flowers and leaves with strokes of white, or add shading with deeper intensities of color.

To begin, mix a small amount of green and yellow paint. With a fine-tip brush, fill in the leaves and stems. Highlight them with a mixture of yellow and white paint; outline them and add veins to the leaves with brown.

The flowers may be painted in any shade desired. Outline the flowers first, then lighten the paint with drops of white and fill in the flowers with the lighter shade.

Fill in the letters with light blue. Brush white over each letter and outline it with red. Fill in the small heart at the bottom with red, highlight it along the top curved edges with white, and outline it with blue dots.

Around the edge of the wooden heart, paint a narrow rim of blue. Inside it, add a border of blue dots.

To add an antique finish to the heart, apply antiquing stain evenly with a brush. With a clean rag, wipe off almost all the stain from the center. Around the edges, wipe off the excess, leaving a light glaze. Using a clean brush, stroke from the center out, feathering the stain toward the edges. Let it dry overnight.

Give the heart a rustic look by rubbing it vigorously with a cloth dipped in turpentine.

To weatherproof the heart, apply several layers of varnish, sanding lightly between coats.

Add a metal hanger to the back.

1 Square = 1 Inch

"To Have a Friend, Be One"
♥ NEEDLEPOINT SAMPLER

Signifying love, faith, and good luck, this Pennsylvania Dutch design is the perfect background for a sentiment of friendship. To complete the 14x21-inch stitchery, follow the colored pattern on pages 76-77.

MATERIALS
20x27 inches of 10-mesh needlepoint canvas
3-ply yarn in the following colors: red, dark orange, yellow, light and dark blue, light and dark green, white
Tapestry needle; artist's stretcher strips

INSTRUCTIONS
Before you begin stitching, bind the edges of the needlepoint canvas with masking tape to prevent raveling and stretch the canvas on a frame or stretcher bars.

To begin stitching, locate the center on the pattern, pages 76-77, and on the canvas. Beginning at this point, stitch the saying, using three strands of the yarn and basket-weave stitches.

Work the outline of the large heart next; fill it in completely. Continue stitching the outlines of the shapes and filling them in. Work a 1½-inch-wide white border around the design.

To block the completed needlepoint, cut a piece of plywood larger than the canvas. Attach a piece of quilt batting to the board, then cover it with gingham fabric, keeping the grain of the fabric as straight as possible.

Dampen the canvas and, with T-pins, mount it on the board. Align the corners and edges of the canvas with the gingham squares.

Sprinkle the canvas with water and let it dry at least 24 hours. Then remove it from the board and press it lightly on the back with a warm iron.

1 Square = 1 Stitch

"Love and Kisses"
♥ **NEEDLEPOINT TOY**

For a tot or a teen, this mother rabbit and her baby bunny is an ideal gift. The needlepoint toy stands 16 inches high when stitched on 12-count canvas as shown. (You can change the size by working the design on larger- or smaller-count canvas.)

Stitch the toy in pastel wool yarn, then add your own touches of whimsy—a few string whiskers, a bow for Mother Rabbit's bonnet, or a lace edging for her apron skirt.

MATERIALS
16x22 inches of No. 12-count
  needlepoint canvas
One 40-yard skein each of Elsa
  Williams tapestry yarn (or
  a suitable substitute) in
  the colors listed in the color
  key, *below*
½ yard of pink fabric
½ yard of ½-inch-wide lace
1½ yards of ¼-inch-diameter
  cable cord
Polyester fiberfill
String
10-inch length of ribbon
Needlepoint frame or artist's
  stretcher strips
Tapestry needle

INSTRUCTIONS
Before you begin stitching, bind the edges of the needlepoint canvas with masking tape. To minimize distortion of the canvas as you work, mount it on artist's stretcher strips or a frame.

Cut the yarn in 18- to 20-inch lengths and use a yarn caddy to keep strands sorted by color. (*Note:* You will need very little of the navy blue, black, and gray yarns. Use scraps of yarn you have on hand, if desired.)

As you stitch, maintain even tension so the yarn completely covers the canvas and the stitches appear uniform.

To begin stitching, follow the color key and charts, *below* and *on page 80.* Use basket-weave stitches for large areas of color, and continental stitches for outlining and small areas of color. Work the baby rabbit's tail in turkey loops, then clip the loops close to the canvas.

When the needlepoint is completed, tack lace along the bottom of the apron. To add whiskers to the mother rabbit, cut six 3-inch lengths of string. Thread each string on a needle, knot one end, and pull the string through to the right side.

Tape the strings to the front of the needlepoint to keep them out of the seam allowance as you stitch the toy together.

To assemble the toy, trim the needlepoint canvas ½ inch beyond the outer row of stitching, creating a seam allowance.

From pink fabric, cut a backing the same size as the needlepoint front, an oval piece (gusset) that measures 4 inches across at the widest point and 8 inches at the longest point, and enough bias strips to cover the cable cord.

Stitch the bias strips together and sew them over the cable cord, using a zipper foot. Pin this piping along the edges of the stitched canvas so it is just inside the first row of needlepoint stitches. Baste in place.

With right sides together, pin the needlepoint front to the fabric back, matching raw edges. With a zipper foot, stitch just inside the first row of needlepoint stitches, sewing as close to the piping as possible. Leave the bottom open.

Turn the toy right side out to check that the piping is in place and no bare canvas is exposed in the seams. Then turn it wrong side out again, and clip curves.

To stitch the gusset to the toy, first stay-stitch ⅜ inch from the edges of the gusset and clip the curves. With right sides facing, pin the gusset to the bottom of the toy, easing to fit. Stitch, using a ½-inch seam allowance, and leaving an opening for turning. Clip the curves.

Turn the toy right side out and stuff it firmly with fiberfill. Slipstitch the opening closed.

Finally, stiffen the whiskers with paraffin or candle wax and trim them to about 2 inches. Add a ribbon bow to the mother rabbit's bonnet, if desired.

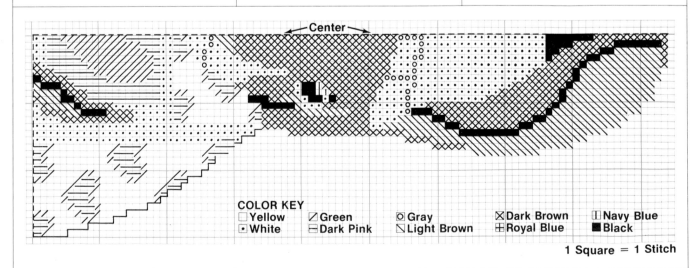

COLOR KEY

☐ Yellow	☑ Green	⊙ Gray	☒ Dark Brown	Ⅱ Navy Blue
⊡ White	⊟ Dark Pink	◺ Light Brown	⊞ Royal Blue	■ Black

1 Square = 1 Stitch

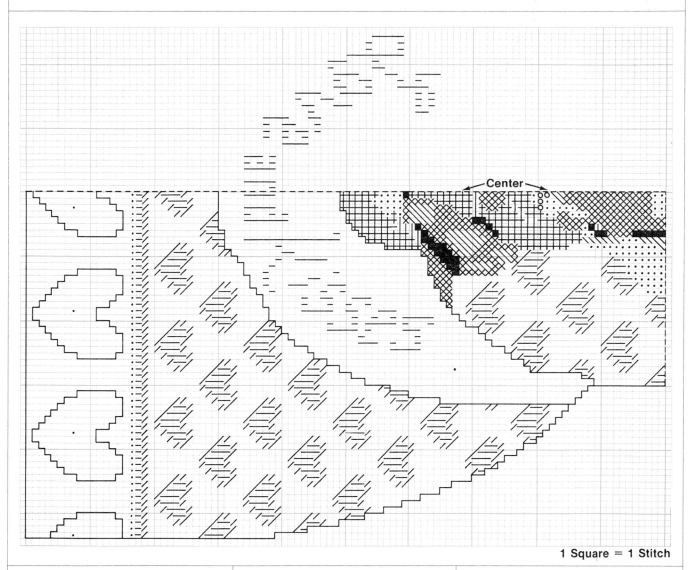

← Center →

1 Square = 1 Stitch

ACKNOWLEDGMENTS

Designers
Holly Adams—basket, 24
Ginger Bassett—edging, 36
Mary Lamb Becker—hat, 17
Jenny Blethen—cross-stitch, 20
Marlene Burnell—bouquet, 7
Linda DeMichele-Price—paper
  baskets, 54
Phyllis Dunstan—sachets, 9;
  hearts-and-flowers trims, 49
Elizabeth Eakins for The Collec-
  tor's Choice, New York, NY—
  braided rug, 46
Linda Emmerson—place mats,
  29; note cards, 54
Dixie Falls—afghan, 29
Debbie Felton—ribbon trims, 49
Dorothy Heiscy—baby quilt, 26
Shirley J. Hewlett—quilt, 34-35
Laura Holtorf—stocking, 57;
  needlepoint sampler, 74-75

Rebecca Jerdee—candlesticks, 63
Laura Kluvo—pocket heart, 49
Ann Marie Kocherga—papier-
  mâché ornaments, 53
Pat Kraus—folk art pillow, 23
Barbara Krumhardt—chair, 29
Ann Levine—pillow, 70
Marion Leyds—tatted heart, 5, 49
Nancy Lindemeyer—wreath, 33
Mimi McLellan—lampshades, 41
Pipka for Pipka's Workshop, Min-
  neapolis, MN—painted sign, 72
Richard Rabanus—box, 25
Mimi Shimmin—woodburning, 6
Sara Jane Treinen—crocheted
  ornament, 49; sampler, 74-75
Ciba Vaughan—cut-paper cards,
  4-5; candy box, 6; feather
  wreath heart, 49; wreath, 60
James Williams—pansy, 4, 49;
  cross-stitched card, 5; frame, 8;
  pocket, 15; cradle, 45; wreath,
  63; sampler, 65; toy, 78

Photographers
Mike Dieter—24, 54
Hedrich-Blessing—15, 19, 23, 33,
  46, 74-75
Thomas Hooper—9, 20
William Hopkins—7, 26, 29, 31,
  34-35, 36, 38, 57, 62-63, 70, 72
Scott Little—cover, 4-5, 6, 8, 14,
  17, 28, 41, 48-49, 53, 60, 64-65, 78
Perry Struse—25, 43, 45

*For their cooperation and courtesy,
we extend a special thanks to:*
C. M. Offray & Sons, Inc.—belt
  and bag, 19
Becky Senti for Country Sampler,
  Ltd., Story City, IA—quilt, 43